A Little Porch Time

Quilts with a Touch of Southern Hospitality

By Lynda Hall

A Little Porch Time

Quilts with a Touch of Southern Hospitality

By Lynda Hall

A Little Porch Time

Quilts with a Touch of Southern Hospitality

By Lynda Hall

Edited by Judy Pearlstein

Design by Brian Grubb

Photographs by Aaron Leimkuehler

Illustrations by Lon Eric Craven

Production Assistance by Jo Ann Groves

Location photos at Missouri Town 1855, Jackson County Parks & Recreation, www.jacksongov.org

Published by Kansas City Star Books
1729 Grand Boulevard
Kansas City, Missouri 64108

First edition, first printing
ISBN: 978-1-935362-41-8.
Library of Congress number: 2010927144

Printed in the United States of America
By Walsworth Publishing Co.
Marceline, Missouri

To order copies, call StarInfo, 816-234-4636 (say "Operator)

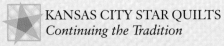

KANSAS CITY STAR QUILTS
Continuing the Tradition

The Quilter's Home Page

Table of Contents

It's not what we know, but who we know that makes all the difference in our lives. I feel extremely honored that I get to meet such wonderful people daily. When I was growing up I remember my dad saying, "When you go to bed at night, count your blessings. If you can look back through the day and cannot think of one new thing you learned that day, you know it all." I've never been able to do that. So, it's with heartfelt gratitude that I thank all the people who have come into and stayed, or just passed through my life, for teaching me new things every day.

Acknowledgements

I remember a very important lesson from my mom. She always said a THANK-YOU goes a long way, so:

Thank you to my mom and dad for being such wonderful role models, for guiding me through my younger years, always teaching me to try new things and to learn from the mistakes I made, for teaching me to be the best I can be. My dad died when he was only 54. That taught me, at a young age, to enjoy life. My mom is 87 and when I grow up I hope to be just like her.

All my love and devotion goes to my wonderful husband, Curt, who has been by my side for over 41 years. He's always backed my creative endeavors and always believed in me. Thank you for being there ALWAYS! I love you!

As a mother of two sons, Chad and Bryan, I couldn't have asked for two better little boys who were such a delight to us while they were growing up, nor more proud of the young men they have become.

To Lane and Chelsie, our daughter-in-laws, who share our lives. We are so happy you are a part of our family and that you take such good care of our sons.

I am one of the luckiest women I know with two wonderful granddaughters, Rebecca and Sarah, who live so close and share their lives with us. And, I'm excited to say we will have a baby boy join our family this December. Congratulations Chad and Lane. Being a mommy and daddy is one of the greatest joys.

A very special thank you to my sister-in-law and best friend, Donna Phillips, for all her help stitching on the wool projects for this book. Here's to all the days we have spent together laughing, stitching, lunches at our favorite places and, oh yes, let's not forget our 5:00 gab fests!

To Barbara McCauley, owner of Apopka Quilt Company, who machine quilted the quilt for this book "A Little Porch Time." I'm so happy you have a long arm and that you are close to me! Here's to future projects!

It's with a ton of gratitude to my friend, Edie McGinnis, for introducing me to Diane McLendon and Doug Weaver at The Kansas City Star.

To Diane and Doug for thinking my idea for this book had merit.

My gratitude also extends to everyone that worked on my book. I wish I could have been there to see how all of you operate, but please know you have made me look wonderful with all your help and expertise.

Judy Pearlstein, my editor, for keeping me on the straight and narrow and for editing my book so it still sounds like who I am. Thank you also for putting up with my less than stellar computer knowledge.

To Brian Grubb, book designer, for all his hard work and making everything look like how I love my quilts to look with that old time feeling that comes through just perfectly.

To Aaron Leimkuehler, photographer, for all the beautiful shots you took for the book. Oh, how I wish I could have been there seeing you do your magic.

To Christina DeArmond, tech editor, who deserves all kinds of kudos for checking my math and making it all wonderful.

I want to thank Moda Fabrics for donating fabric and Weeks Dye Works for donating thread. Thank you to Quilter's Station in Lee's Summit, Missouri, The Country Sampler in Spring Green,

Wisconsin, The Buggy Barn in Reardon, Washington, and Quilts on Plum Lane in Dade City, Florida for kitting my patterns.

A special Thank-you to the Missouri Town folks, who so graciously agreed for the photography of this book to take place in such a wonderful community. (Editor's note: Thank you to Gordon, Gary, Don, Linda and Mark for being so nice and for making our job easier.)

Lastly, I would like to take this opportunity to say, thank you, to my sister, Sharron. Although we are unable to sew together any longer, you are in my thoughts each and every day. I know the "me" is still watching over the "shadow."

Dedication

I would like to dedicate my book to my mother, Edna Parton, who is 87 years young. She's a mom, a best friend and a person who instilled in me a strong sense of family. She's a gentle person whom everyone loves. She's guided me through my life by standing beside me, never demanding or unkind. For many years she worked beside me doing all the appliqué on the quilts for my pattern line – Primitive Pieces by Lynda. Thank you so much Mom, I love you.

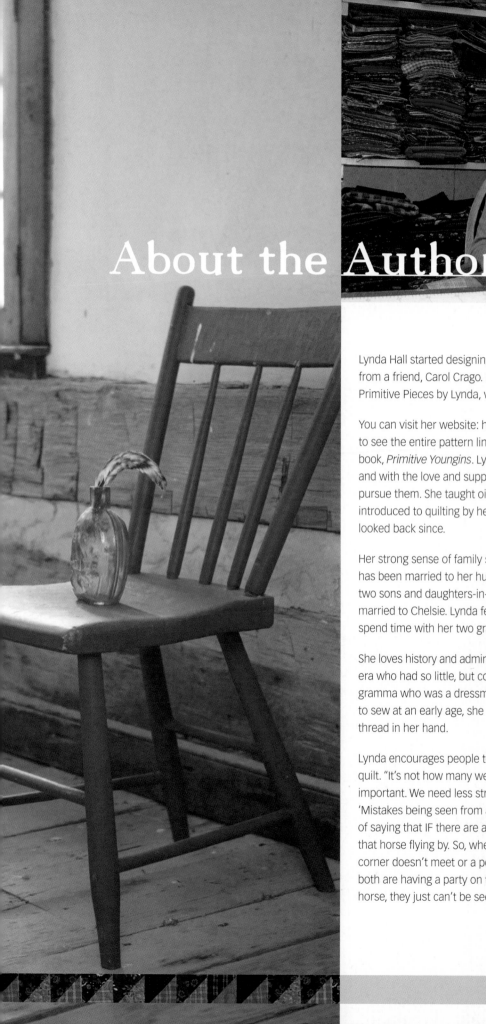

About the Author

Lynda Hall started designing quilts in 1999 after encouragement from a friend, Carol Crago. Her own quilt pattern company, Primitive Pieces by Lynda, was born in 2001.

You can visit her website: http://www.primitivepiecesbylynda.com to see the entire pattern line, which consists of 71 patterns and a book, *Primitive Youngins*. Lynda has always loved creative endeavors and with the love and support of her family, she's been able to pursue them. She taught oil painting for 15 years. In 1991, she was introduced to quilting by her sister-in-law, Donna Phillips, and hasn't looked back since.

Her strong sense of family shows in each of her patterns. She has been married to her husband, Curtis for 41 years. They have two sons and daughters-in-law: Chad, married to Lane, and Bryan, married to Chelsie. Lynda feels like a lucky "gramma," getting to spend time with her two granddaughters, Rebecca and Sarah.

She loves history and admires the women from her grandmother's era who had so little, but could accomplish so much. Having had a gramma who was a dressmaker and a mom who showed her how to sew at an early age, she feels right at home with a needle and thread in her hand.

Lynda encourages people to enjoy the process of making each quilt. "It's not how many we make, it's the fun we have that is important. We need less stress and more fun in our lives. 'Mistakes being seen from a galloping horse,' is a quilter's way of saying that IF there are any mistakes, it won't be seen from that horse flying by. So, when you make your next quilt and a corner doesn't meet or a point comes up missing – perhaps both are having a party on the back or from that galloping horse, they just can't be seen. Enjoy!"

Introduction

I like sitting on the porch, with my first cup of coffee, early in the morning. The sky is a beautiful shade of blue as the sun comes up over the horizon to the east. All the critters are gathering their breakfast. They are squawking, probably at their young, just like we would do while getting our kids to hurry up for school. I love watching some of the birds take their morning bath. Others prefer an evening bath. Sometimes they'll be lined up to take a turn. The cardinals are beautiful in their red coats, while the blue jay's blue rivals the color of the sky. You can't help but love the crows that carry on so when chatting with each other. They love to sit in the sycamore tree the best. I like to make up stories about what they might be talking and think it's really gossip they are sharing with each other. The squirrels chase each other up, down and around all the trees. The bees are humming around the flowers and, oh my, what a sight the butterflies make when they show up. Usually I see the little yellow sulfurs chasing each other first. There are two pairs of them that live near us, but it's not long before the parade begins. You see, I started a butterfly garden this past year and it's brought a colorful array of flying colors to our yard. Zebra swallowtails, tiger swallowtails, zebra longwings, giant skippers and even some queens, just to mention a few. How can you not like waking up to that?

When I designed the *A Little Porch Time* quilt (page 12), I used a lot of the things I can see from my front porch. The old watering can really doesn't hold water any longer, but that spout is worth a second glance as I sit on the porch. The cabin you see in the quilt represents a dream down the road for Pa and me. The sunflower block down in the right hand corner was the very first quilt block I ever designed for my pattern company, Primitive Pieces by Lynda, back in 2001. I was driving down our country road when I saw the most gorgeous sunflowers climbing up to reach the sky by an old fence. I bet their stalks were six feet tall or better. Of course, I had to have some for myself so I planted some skyscrapers too. They reminded me of my great Aunt Robena, who was affectionately called Auntie Bean by everyone in the family. I just had to have a sunflower quilt named after her. The sunflower block is in the bottom right corner of *A Little Porch Time*.

The larger hand, down in the left hand corner is mine and the smaller ones represent our little girls, Rebecca and Sarah, our granddaughters. I'm holding their hearts in my hand just like a gramma should.

I planted all different kinds of flowers to attract butterflies. I don't have much of a green thumb, but what I planted survived and we had a butterfly parade all summer long. Did you know that if you call "butterfly?" they will come close to you? That's probably not really true, but one day the kids were in their wading pool and we saw some butterflies in the yard. I told Rebecca to call them and they'd come over. She did and they did and so now she thinks gramma can talk with the butterflies.

Topaz, our kitty, is also in the quilt. She watched this one coming together and nagged and nagged until I put her in it. As soon as I laid the quilt down on the floor to see how it was looking, she was on the quilt and very excited to see her image there by the watering can. I tell her she's my quilting partner, so it only seemed right to have her on the quilt.

I love collecting baskets, so there had to be some of them as well. I'm in love with how the old ones look and it also reminds me of my gramma. She'd go out each day to gather fruits and vegetables from her garden. She had a wonderful gathering basket for just that purpose. The Flying Geese you see in the quilt are a reminder of where I was born. We lived in Canada for such a short period of time after I was born, but it's where my mom and dad lived as children growing up. We moved to Florida when I was very young. We don't have the Canadian geese flying here where I live, but I can look at the quilt to be reminded of them. The Nine Patch and Shoo Fly blocks are favorites and fun to make. The Sawteeth seem to be a signature of mine because I love using them in borders. These are smaller, but never-the-less, needed to be in this quilt.

Some of the items you see in the Porch Time quilt are repeated again in the small wool projects. They seemed to take on a whole new meaning and with each project there's a fun story to tell you as well.

I hope you enjoy making *A Little Porch Time* and that you spend some time on your porch breathing in all the inspiration that surrounds you too.

Sewing Tips

Fabric Applique

I especially love needle turn. It's what I learned to do when I first started quilting. Please use the method you feel the most comfortable with.

If you use the needle turn method please note that there is a drawing line, which will become your finished size. Cut approximately ⅛" to ¼" more than this drawn line so that you can turn it under.

When possible, appliqué onto the smaller sections before sewing the different sections together. It makes it much easier to do.

Wool Applique

I learned to stitch wool down using a primitive stitch. I love the way it looks. I'm not a big fan of the buttonhole stitch, or of every stitch showing, so I try to match the color of the item I am stitching down, not the color I'm stitching it to.

The wool primitive stitch is nothing more than a big appliqué stitch. When stitching on fabrics, you want to take smaller stitches and just catch the piece at the outside edge. This way the stitch will not be seen. Here's how to do the primitive stitch:

1. Thread your needle and knot the end.

2. Anchor your thread between the layers – the piece being appliquéd down and the background piece. This way it will not show on the back.

3. Use an appliqué stitch, or a blind hem stitch, only you take a larger bite out of the piece you are sewing down. Because wool can ravel, you will need to have at least a ⅛" to ¼" bite out of the wool.

I usually have my stitches ¼" apart.

Applique stitch on the wool fabrics.

Measuring

We all sew a little differently. Measure as you go and make any adjustments you need to. Since this quilt is done in strips, A through E, the main objective of the background is that each strip measure the same.

When measuring for the borders, always measure down/across through the middle of your quilt to get an accurate measurement for each border.

Color

I love working with color. I hear from a lot of people that they don't feel comfortable putting colors together. Learning a few rules will keep it all in perspective for you.

- There are only six colors that WE ALL USE
- 3 primary colors – red, yellow, blue
- When you mix two primary colors together you get:
- 3 secondary colors – green, purple, orange.

Every piece of fabric you have must fall into one of those 6 color groups. (Pink is not a color by itself, it's only red with white added to it so it goes in the red group. Brown is not a color by itself, it's only yellow made darker so it goes into the yellow group. Rust is not a color by itself, it's dark orange so goes into the orange group. If you are looking at a multi-color-piece of fabric, think about the one that is most prominent and put it in that color group.

There is a 3rd group - BUT, it only means you've mixed a primary and a secondary color together - they are called tertiary colors. In other words a two word color: Orange/red, blue/green, blue/purple. The tertiary colors also go into one of the six color groups. If you do this with all of your fabrics your color combinations will be so much better. Use complimentary colors. They are opposites on a color wheel: red - green, blue - orange, yellow – purple. When you have a two word color you need a two word compliment: green/yellow - red/purple, orange/red - blue/green, purple/red - yellow/green

- Black and white are not colors.

- If you use all six colors in a quilt – they WILL all go together.

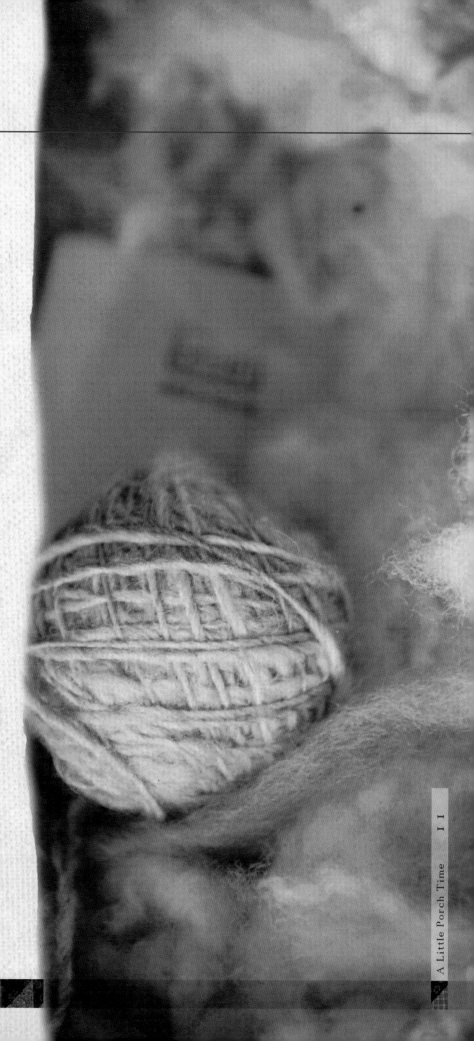

Most important.….It's the VALUE of the colors you use that make a quilt look different. Value means from light to dark, on a scale from one to ten - one being the lightest, ten being the darkest.

Templates

All templates are provided. A ¼" seam allowance needs to be added when cutting out the shapes for fabric. When using wool, no seam allowance is needed.

Cutting

Wool – cut background pieces slightly larger than the finished size. Wool can stretch or ravel a bit. You can trim it down to the correct size later. REMEMBER to leave at least ½" around the edge for this purpose.

When cutting wool for your appliqué pieces, the drawing line and the cutting line are the same.

Thread

You can use any thread you would like for these projects. The important thing to remember is to use colors that match the piece you are sewing down, not what you are sewing it to. I love Weeks Dye Works 6-ply thread. The colors are yummy and the variety is the best I've seen.

I also use wool thread – Aurifil and Genziana are my favorites.

I like to use wool thread on larger pieces. It's thicker and looks really nice, but on small pieces it's almost too much thread, so I prefer using one strand of the Weeks Dye Works thread for them.

When you have layers of wool to sew together, like a flower that is layered, sew the center of the flower to the larger piece of the flower before you sew the entire piece to the background. It makes it much easier.

QUILT SIZE: 78 3/4" X 77 1/2"

SAMPLER QUILT WITH AN
ASSORTMENT OF BLOCKS,
SASHINGS AND BORDERS.

Designed and stitched by Lynda Hall

Machine quilted by Barbara McCauley, Apopka Quilt Company

Pleae read all the instructions before you begin.

See the diagram on page 14 showing the entire quilt. Some of the sections are pieced and some are background squares that will be used for your appliqué. I pieced this quilt together in strips starting at the bottom right hand corner. The drawing shows the different blocks and strips, i.e. row A, block 1 (Auntie Bean's Stalk block). Please refer to this when you are sewing the different sections together.

Materials to Gather Together

- 4 yards assortment of middle value colors for the center section blocks, Nine Patch, Shoo Fly and Sawteeth sections of the quilt. I chose to piece together an assortment of plaids: green, red, middle value yellow (brown). Each of these plaids is very grayed down.

- 1 yard black with stars for the inner borders

(Two of the borders are 4" wide and two are 1" wide pieced together.)

- 2 yards of a middle value red plaid for the outer borders. This is also very grayed down and pieced together.

Auntie Bean's Stalk block
- ¼ yard assortment of red prints, plaids, stripes
- ¼ yard assortment of middle value yellows
- ¼ yard assortment of blacks

Watering can - ½ yard assortment of grays – gray with black stars and/or plaid

Beehive colors – scraps of red, green, blue, light yellow (cream) and dark orange (sienna)

Leaves and stems – 1 yard total of an assortment of greens – middle value to dark

Flowers – fat eighths of assorted colors – red, green, blue, orange, purple, dark yellow (brown)

Large basket – 1 fat quarter dark gray stripe fabric.

Smaller baskets –1 fat quarter each – red, blue, dark yellow (brown)

Cat – fat quarter black

House – 1 fat eighth of dark orange (sienna)/black plaid for one section
- 1 fat eighth dark sienna plaid for other section
- 1 fat eighth gray for the roof
- scraps of 3 different fabrics for windows and doors

3 hands – 3 different fat eighths of light yellow (cream)

Geese – 1 fat quarter assortment of blacks
- 1 fat quarter background fabrics for the side pieces

Birds – 1 fat quarter total of assorted browns and black (Use background fabrics for wings.)

Star – scraps of light blue for house, brown for the larger one in the basket

Butterflies – scraps of yellow for the wings, black for the bodies

Templates begin on page 39

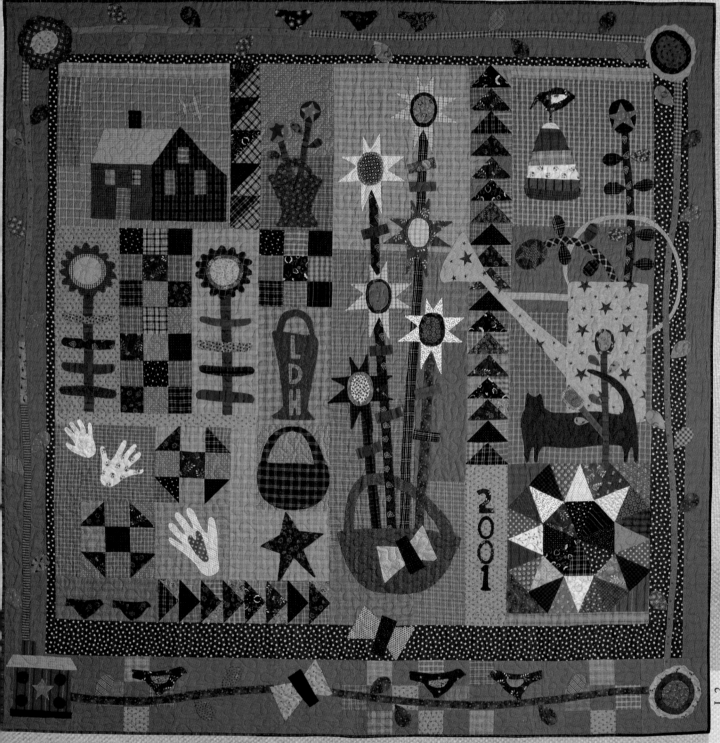

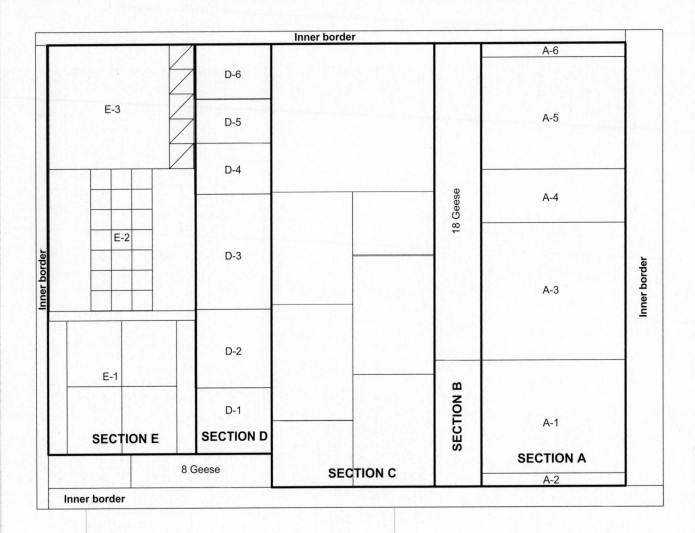

Inner border

E-3

D-6

D-5

D-4

E-2

D-3

18 Geese

A-6

A-5

A-4

A-3

A-1

A-2

SECTION B

SECTION A

E-1

D-2

D-1

SECTION E

SECTION D

SECTION C

8 Geese

Inner border

Inner border

Inner border

Section A

17" x 62 ³⁄₄" finished

Block A1, Auntie Bean's Stalks

Cut:

- 8 black A pieces

- 8 yellow A pieces

- 16 red A pieces

- 4 green B pieces

Begin by sewing the cut triangles into a larger triangle shape. Sew a red triangle onto each side of the yellow triangle. Then sew a black triangle on the bottom of the yellow triangle. It will look like this.

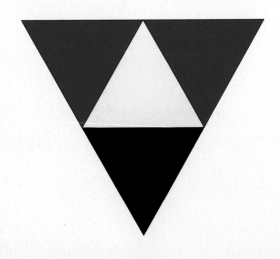

Make 8 of these units for your block. Sew 4 of these units together making one half of your block. Sew the other 4 units together to make the second half. Check the center edge to make sure you have a straight line. You might need to trim ONLY the black triangles a scant amount. If they are not straight they will bunch in the middle. Sew the two sides together and you have your sunflower. Sew on the 4 corners (Template B) and your block is complete. You will have a 17 ½" block.

The remainder of A Section will be background pieces. They are cut as follows:

A2: 2" x 17 ½" Sew onto the bottom of your Auntie Bean's Stalk block.

A3: 17" x 17 ½"

A4: 10" x 17 ½"

A5: 17 ¼" x 17 ½"

A6: 2" x 17 ½"

Sew these pieces together, referring to your drawing: A2, A1, A3, A4, A5, A6

Total strip length: 62 ¾" long

Cut the watering can from two gray pieces:

The can and large spout are from the gray with the black stars fabric.

The handle and connector piece from the can to the spout are the gray plaid.

(Note: add ¼" seam allowance to each of the templates.)

Place the can on top of the A3 and A4 background squares – just above the Auntie Bean's Stalks block.

You can appliqué the can onto this section now. Leave openings for adding the stems later. It's easier to appliqué on smaller pieces than waiting until the quilt is all sewn together. However, the handle and the spout do go over into the other sections so appliqué what you can now and pin the rest of it out of the way until you have more sections sewn together.

The cat and the flower can be appliquéd onto A3 now. The stems are 14" and 6".

The bird and the beehive are in the block at the top – A5. The beehive is pieced together using scraps of red, green, blue, light yellow (cream) and dark orange (sienna). Place the beehive on the left side of your block. Attach the bird on top of the beehive. You will have flowers coming out of your watering can that stretch up into this block. After finishing section A, set it aside for later.

Section B

5" x 62 ¾" finished

Geese unit

Piece together 26 geese. I like them to be really scrappy so you will have leftovers from your squares that you cut. Use these in the other sections.

Cut 7 – 6 ¼" squares, cut them diagonally twice to make 4 black triangles.

Cut 26 – 3 ⅜" squares, cut once diagonally to make two triangles for the side pieces.

Sew 18 geese units together for this section and save the remainder for later. Point your geese towards the top of your quilt.

To the bottom of this 18-geese unit, sew a strip of background fabric – 5 ½" x 18 ¼". Appliqué a date that is important to you here in this space. I chose 2001 because that's the year I started my pattern company. You can sew this Section B strip onto the left side of your Section A strip now.

Cut a strip of the black star border fabric – 4 ½" wide x the length of your Section A strip – 63 ¼"

(Tip: Before making this strip, please measure yours to make sure it's this size. We all sew a little differently, so pre-measuring your own will save any errors in cutting)

Sew this strip to the right side of your Section A. You are now able to appliqué the curved handle of your watering can down.

Section C

16" x 62 ¾" finished

This section is where your large basket is and where your star flowers will grow.

Cut and piece together this section that will be 16 ½" wide x 63 ¼" long. You can piece this section any way you'd like or have it just be only one fabric. I'll leave that up to you.

To cut it like mine: cut the top block 21" x 16 ½".

For the left side, from top down, cut the first piece 17 ¼" x 8 ½". Cut the next piece 17" x 8 ½". Cut the bottom left piece 9 ½" x 8 ½".

On the right, cut the first piece down from the top block 9 ¾" x 8 ½". Cut the second piece 17" x 8 ½". Cut the bottom piece 16 ½" x 8 ½".

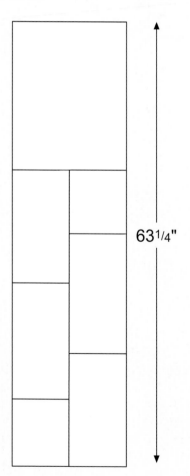

63¹/₄"

- After piecing the background as you want it, Cut out your large basket using the dark gray stripe fabric and place it approximately 3 ½" up from the bottom of this panel.

- Cut 6 star flowers – a template is provided.

    4 light backgrounds with 4 dark centers

    2 dark backgrounds with 2 light centers

- Cut green stems 1 ¼" wide using an assortment of green fabrics. The longest is 47". The middle one is 41", and the smallest is 18". You can have each one be different greens or piece together the stems using an assortment of fabrics. Place the flowers where you want them to be. Make sure some of the stems are on top of the handle of your basket and some under it to make it look more dimensional.

I would appliqué this section before adding it to the Sections A and B. When you do have all three sections together, you will be able to finish the appliqué of the watering can spout. It does come all the way over to this panel.

Section D

9" x 57 ³/₄" finished

This section consists of background squares on which you will be appliquéing the star, different sized baskets and the flowers you'll put in the top basket. Cut two stems 4" and 6" long. There is also a Nine Patch block in this strip.

D1: 9" x 9 ½"

D2: 10 ½" x 9 ½"

D3: 13 ½" x 9 ½"

D4: Nine Patch block – Cut 3 ½" squares, 5 black, 4 light backgrounds. Sew together as shown on page 18.

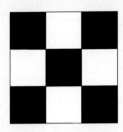

D5: 9" x 9 ½"

D6: 9 ¼" x 9 ½"

Total length of Section D, at this point is 57 ¾".

- The star is appliquéd onto D1.

- The fat round basket is appliquéd onto D2.

- The long basket is appliquéd onto D3.

- The Nine Patch block is D4.

- The small basket with flowers is appliquéd onto D5 and D6.

DO NOT sew this section onto the previous section at this time.

Section E

24" x 57 ¾ " finished

Piece together the remaining geese units (8) just as you did previously. The points will face to the right. Set aside until Section E is finished.

Block E1

The Shoo Fly block and hand blocks

Make 2 Shoo Fly blocks:

- 4 – 3 ⅞" black squares, cut once diagonally to make 2 triangles each.

- Cut 4 – 3 ⅞" background squares, cut once diagonally to make 2 triangles each.

- Cut 2 – 3 ½" black squares.

- Cut 8 – 3 ½" background squares.

This will make 2 Shoo Fly blocks as shown.

- Cut 2 – 9 ½" squares of background fabric. Offset the Shoo Fly blocks with these background squares. Cut 3 ¼" x 18 ½" strips. Sew one on to each side of this block.

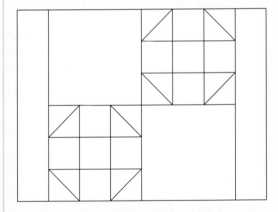

Appliqué the adult hand, with the heart in the center, in the bottom right hand corner. Appliqué the bigger of the two children's hands in the upper right hand corner and let the smaller child's hand go out into that strip you sewed onto the left hand side.

Block E2

Zinnias with Nine Patch

Make the two Nine Patch blocks.

- Cut 10 black 3 ½" squares.

- Cut 11 background 3 ½" fabric squares.

- Sew 5 black squares and 4 background fabric squares together in rows of 3 to make your Nine Patch blocks.

- Sew 3 background squares together making an extra row to sew between your nine patch blocks as shown in the picture.

- Sew a strip 7 ¾" x 21" to each side of your Nine Patch strip.

Cut a strip of background fabric 2 ¼" x 24. Sew this to the bottom of your zinnia/Nine Patch block.

Appliqué the zinnia flowers onto each of the side pieces shown above. Cut zinnia stems 18" long. Trim as desired. These side pieces are not drawn to scale. They are only to show you placement.

Block E3

The block at the top left corner will be the cabin. Cut a square that measures 18 ½" x 20 ½". Appliqué the cabin and small star onto this block.

Sawteeth Squares

Cut 5 – 4 ³/₈" black and 5 – 4 ³/₈" light squares (to make each one different) and cut each one in half once diagonally. There will be leftovers.

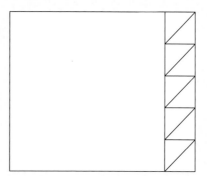

To make the Sawteeth, sew one black triangle to one light triangle. Sew together to make 5 squares You will need 5 blacks and 5 background fabrics to make these Sawteeth. Sew onto the right side of cabin square.

After you have made each of the blocks in section E, sew them together. Sew Section E and Section D together.

To finish the bottom of sections E and D, sew the remaining 8 Geese that you made earlier to a background strip that measures 5 ½" x 13". Appliqué two little birds facing to the right in this section before you add the borders.

Borders

I love seeing the borders different sizes. It sets your quilt apart from all the others that measure each border the same. Having your quilt just a little off center always makes for a fun picture. The focal point of your quilt doesn't always have to be exactly in the center.

Each of us sews a little differently so border lengths are not always the same. Always measure across/down through the middle of your quilt to get the correct measurement for the width and/or length for each border you sew on.

Cut the first bottom border 4 ½" x the width of the top. Stitch.

Cut the left side and top small first border 1 ½" (1" finished size) x the length/width and stitch to the top and the side.

Cut the larger borders as follows:

- Top – 6 ¼" x the width of your top

- Right size – 3 ½" x the length of your top

- Bottom – 9" x the width of your top

- Left side – 5 ¼" x the length of your top

After all the borders are on you can choose how much or how little you want to appliqué on.

Here's what I did to complete my quilt.

- Across the top, there is the vine with 9 leaves, three small birds and a large flower in each corner. Cut vines 71" to 75" long and trim to fit.

- Down the right hand side, there is the vine with 8 leaves, and the completed portion of the watering can handle. (I chose to have the vines weave in and out of the handle.)

- Across the bottom there are vines, 7 leaves, 3 birds – two facing right and one facing left.

- In the bottom left hand corner is a bird house, and in the right hand corner a large flower.

- Up the left hand side is a vine with 8 leaves.

- There are 3 butterflies that are near the bottom center, one in the bottom border, one in the black bottom border and one on the big basket.

- The cat is standing at the base of the watering can. There are 2 middle sized flowers, stems and leaves between the watering can and the cat.

- There are 2 medium sized flowers, stems and leaves coming out of the watering can. The curved one on the left is 14", the other is 19".

- LDH was appliquéd in the long basket in Section D. Add your own initials to make it yours.

Back

One of the things that always makes me happy is to be able to crawl under a quilt that is scrappy. Since the front is that way, it only seems fitting to me that the back should be scrappy too. Using some of the pieces left over from the front or some other fabrics that coordinate with what is in the quilt, piece the back. Here are a few ideas to help you out.

1. From fat quarters, make 16" or 18" squares. Sew enough across and/or down to make a back.

2. Since there are Nine Patches on the front – you could make enough Nine Patches using the fat quarters to fill up the back. Cut 10" light and dark squares and sew the squares together into Nine Patch blocks. You could make sashing strips to go between your Nine Patches.

3. There are some very fun prints out there that relate to gardens. Perhaps some with gardening tools would make it look fun, or a bird print.

4. Randomly piece different colored fabrics you've used on the front in no particular order. This is one of my favorite methods. It looks great and uses up some of your stash.

5. Make large geese to sew across through the middle and/or down through the middle of the quilt. Perhaps both ways would look good.

6. Sawteeth down one side of the quilt are always good too.

Layer the top, batting and backing and quilt as desired.

Whatever you decide to do, make it your own and make it fun. After all, you are probably the one that will crawl under it.

I hope you enjoy making *A Little Porch Time*. I also hope, when you do, you'll share your porch with me. (E-mail to Piecemaker51@aol.com.) I love receiving pictures of what you make.

The day is winding down and soon all the critters will be enjoying the evening with their families. We'll all gather again in the morning to start a new day. Until next time…

The Fairy Game

It's most unlikely you would see a bird sitting on top of a beehive, especially a working one. But in my world of primitive, anything goes. Thinking of bees reminds me of a story about our granddaughter, Rebecca. At one family gathering, she wanted to go outside and look for fairies. She told me it was a game. Whoever found the most fairies won! So, being a good gramma, we did just that. We searched high and low for fairies that might be flying around the yard. Becca thought she just might find some in this bird house (not a beehive) sitting on a fence post. She peeked in the hole and didn't see anything. So, she picked up the bird house and shook it. What she encountered was an angry wasp. It flew out of the bird house and stung her on the nose. By the next day, her nose and eyes were all swollen up. She looked a sight for a few days, which warranted lots of hugs and kisses from gramma. We haven't been back out in the yard looking for fairies since. But, we have seen some bees around the flowers and birds flying around the yard.

SIZE: 14" X 20"

WOOL TABLE RUG

Designed by Lynda Hall

Stitched by Donna Phillips & Lynda Hall

Materials to Gather Together

- 1 fat quarter middle value yellow (middle value tan plaid) background fabric
- Scraps of light yellow (beige), red, middle value blue/gray, green, and a multi-plaid of your choice to add texture to the mix for beehive
- 6" square of dark yellow (brown) for the bird
- Scrap of middle value yellow (brown/green) for the wing
- 1 fat quarter middle value green for stems and leaves
- 1 – 4" square each red, blue, purple for the flowers
- 1 fat quarter dark reddish/dark yellow (brown) plaid for the backing

Cutting

Templates for this small project are on pages 45 - 46 Flowers are on page 71.

- Cut your background wool slightly larger than the finished size. You can trim this down later.
- Cut each section of the beehive. The colors are marked on the template. Note: because this is wool, the cutting line and sewing line are the same - no seam allowance is needed.
- Cut 2 – ¼" strips, one 13" long and one 15 ½" long of green for the stems. These are fairly straight so there is no need to cut on the bias.
- Cut out the following for the leaves:

    12 leaves for the left flower, 6 for each side

    7 leaves for the right flower, 3 for the left side,

    4 for the right.
- Cut each piece of the flower using the colors you have chosen.
- Cut the bird and wing.

Assembly

When you are pleased with the presentation, stitch each of the shapes using a primitive stitch.

A little artistic license was taken on this piece. I cut the top left hand corner off. You may choose to leave it on. I will leave that up to you.

When you have completed the appliqué, lay the top and backing together, trim it to the correct size, 14" x 20". If you have chosen to cut the corner off, sew some decorative stitching along that edge. An X stitch was chosen using a wool thread the color of the front. With the back being darker it shows up nicely.

Hold the front and back together using a running stitch, using the color to match the front. Sew approximately ¼" around all sides, even the cut off corner.

Your Fairy Game is now complete. This one is so small that you can make one for yourself and one for a good friend. I know you both will be happy. Enjoy!

Flower Bucket

This watering can no longer holds water, but as stated in the Porch Time quilt, with that spout it's just fun to see when I sit on the porch. The flowers remind me of a story about our youngest granddaughter, Sarah. She started talking at a very young age and with such clarity it's always amazed me. However, there are a few words that are just fun to hear. Each time she walks up on the porch she'll say, "Gramma, your flowders are so pretty." Or, "Can we water your flowders today gramma? Flowers will always remind me of her. And, although there is a hole in the bucket, the birds don't seem to mind. I see them fly up on the porch and perch on the watering can just about every day.

QUILT SIZE: 36" X 24"

|||||||||||||||||||||||||||||||||||||||||||||||||||||||||||||||||||||||||||||||||||||

FABRIC AND WOOL
WALL HANGING OR TABLE RUG

◇◇◇◇◇◇◇◇◇◇◇◇◇◇◇◇◇◇◇◇◇◇◇◇◇◇◇◇◇◇◇◇◇◇

Designed by Lynda Hall

Stitched by Lynda Hall and Donna Phillips

Hand Quilted by Lynda Hall

Materials to Gather Together

- 1 yard assortment of background fabrics - red, middle value yellow (brown) plaids or colors of your choice (same fabrics I used in *Porch Time*)

- 1 fat eighth each – blue, red, orange, black, gray, green, dark yellow (brown), middle value yellow (brown) for Sawteeth

- 1 yard of the same assortment for the backing

- ½ yard of dark blue/gray plaid wool for the watering can, spout and handle

- Scraps of middle value/dark orange, red, light blue, dark blue, purple, green, light/middle yellows, for flowers

- Fat eighth black for 3 small birds

- 1 fat quarter assortment of greens for leaves and stems

- 1 fat quarter each – green stripe and purple plaid for the binding

Cutting the Background

Cut the pieces as follows:

A: 6" x 24 ½"   B: 10 ½" x 12 ½"
C: 10 ½" x 12 ½"   D: 20 ½" x 7 ½"
E: 20 ½" x 5 ½"   F: 8" x 24 ½"
G: Sawteeth square template, p. 69

Piecing the Background
24" x 36"

Start by piecing together the foundation for all your appliqué by using the chart shown left or piece the background as you wish with several different fabrics so that it looks scrappy. *Option: You could also just use one fabric for the background. I'll leave that up to you.*

Once your background or foundation is completed, cut out all the shapes you'll need for the applique.

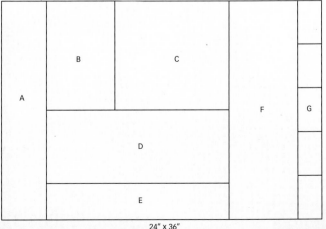

24" x 36"

Cutting Applique Pieces

Some pieces from the Porch Time quilt are repeated in this piece so page numbers are listed below. I used freezer paper to make each of mine.

- Cut 1 watering can, spout and handle. (p. 42 - 43)
- Cut 3 birds. (p. 65)
- Cut 3 sets of the large flower. (Flowers are on p. 69)
- Cut 4 sets of the middle sized flower.
- Cut two stars (one each for two of the flowers).
- Cut 3 small flowers.
- Cut 4 stems 5/8" wide on the bias, 1 – 5" long, 1 – 10", 1 – 16", and 1 – 23" long
- Cut 3 stems ½" wide on the bias, 1 – 3", 1 – 4", and 1 – 16" long
- Cut 2 stems 3/8" wide on the bias, 1 – 4", and 1 – 11" long
- Cut 21 leaves. (p. 69)

Cut 8 triangles to go down the right hand side of your project. I wanted them all to be different so instead of cutting 8 different squares in half and having leftovers, a template is included for this.

Applique

Play with the placement until you are satisfied with the overall presentation. Trim stems as desired. I like to put a spot of glue on each item to keep it in place instead of pinning the pieces down. Applique all the pieces using thread that matches, as closely as you can, to the piece you are sewing down, not to the background color. Use a primitive stitch around each object.

Backing

I pieced the back with the same fabrics I used for the front. The layout is slightly different than the front you see in the chart, but close. ***Note:*** *I had a leftover Nine Patch block from the A Little Porch Time quilt so I incorporated it on the back.* Baste the back, batting and top together to hold everything in place. I hand quilted a 2" grid behind all the applique shapes, including the sawteeth. If you are a machine quilter, yours will be done in no time flat.

Binding

Some people pin the binding down before they sew to keep it in place. I just lay it down on top of the project in the middle of one outside edge, keeping the raw edge to the outside as well, leaving at least an 8" tail, and stitch. When I come to the corner, I stop ¼" from the end, and backstitch. I take it out of the machine, flip the edge up at the corner, then back down on itself, and stitch along that entire edge until I come to the next corner and repeat. When I'm at the end I take it out from the machine, open it up and connect the two ends with a pin where

it will lie flat on top of the project, stitch across where they meet, cut off the excess. I fold it back to the original folded shape and stitch the rest of it in place. It finishes it off just perfectly.

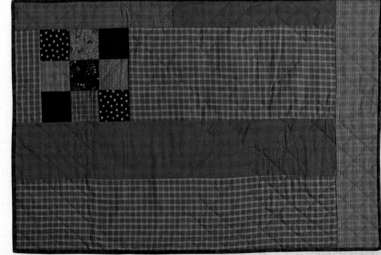

it will lie flat on top of the project, stitch across where they meet, cut off the excess. I fold it back to the original folded shape and stitch the rest of it in place. It finishes it off just perfectly.

You have a completed Flower Bucket of your own to hang on the wall or place on your favorite table.

I hope you enjoy making all the projects in this book. Make them your own by choosing fabrics and colors that make you smile. The most important thing to remember is to have fun while you are stitching. Life is way too short not to enjoy some of the fun things in our lives.

A fun thing I remember about my dad ... He could never remember the names of flowers. Everything to him was a petunia. I had to smile when I was making the flowers for this piece because I always think of my flowers as being hybrids ... that way if they are not drawn correctly I have an excuse for them looking like any other petunia.

Anyone who has a cat on the premises knows how they like to think they run the show. Our kitty, Topaz, is affectionately referred to as the "Queen." There is absolutely no doubt that she runs our household. She was purrfectly happy to note that after all these years, she finally has her own piece to show off. She loved seeing her image on the quilt, but the fact that she has her own small wool piece among the flowers makes her very happy. She informed me it was the cat's meow.

SIZE: 17" X 22"

WOOL WITH FABRIC BINDING

Designed by Lynda Hall

Stitched by Lynda Hall and Donna Phillips

Materials to Gather Together

- 1 fat quarter light yellow (beige) plaid for the background
- 1 fat quarter black for cat
- 1 – 3" square of light yellow for star
- 1 fat eighth of three different purples of light, middle and dark values for flower
- 1 fat eighth of middle value and dark red for flower
- 1 fat eighth of a middle value yellow for flower
- 1 fat eighth of an assortment of greens for 2 stems and leaves, grass and birds wing
- 1 fat eighth of a middle value blue for bird
- 1 fat quarter of a middle value yellow (brown check) for the backing
- 1 fat quarter green/red stripe fabric for binding

A Little Porch Time

32

Cutting

Templates on pages 67 - 68.

- Cut the beige wool plaid background slightly larger than the finished measurement. The reason for this is that sometimes wool can stretch or ravel. I like to cut it slightly larger, then trim it down to size after I've finished all the appliqué.

- Cut 1 black cat and 1 light yellow star.

- Cut two flowers : *(page 63)*

    1 orange/red - large section for left flower

    1 yellow middle section for left flower

    1 dark red center for left flower

    1 dark purple for large section of right flower

    1 middle value blue/purple middle section for right flower

    1 plaid for center of right flower

- Cut 2 – ¼" green stems approximately 12" long. Vary the size per color photo.

- Cut 4 leaves for each flower:

    2 – #1 leaves for left flower

    1 – # 2 leaf for left flower

    1 – # 3 leaf for left flower   *(This is actually only a portion of the leaf. Refer to picture.)*

    1 – #1 leaf for right flower

    2 – #2 leaves for right flower

    1 – #3 leaf for right flower

- Cut a grass strip approximately 16" wide for the bottom.

- Cut 1 blue bird.

- Cut 1 green wing.

- Cut your own initials for the top.

Applique

When you have cut all the pieces for this, placed them, and you are happy with the presentation, appliqué using a primitive stitch. I used a primitive stitch to sew each layer down. See the primitive stitch reference and diagram on page 10.

When you have finished the appliqué, place the front on top of the backing wool you have chosen and trim both at the same time to the desired size – 17" x 22". Cutting both pieces at the same time will keep them the same exact size.

Binding

Cut the striped fabric into 2" strips. (I like to make more binding than I need. Having leftover binding is always the start to another project.) After sewing the strips together, fold them in half and press. After pinning the binding in place, stitch around until you have completed the binding.

You have completed your small wall hanging and/or wool table rug. I hope you've enjoyed making Catnip. Topaz thinks by everyone having one of these, she will be remembered always. That's so much the kitty way.

Auntie Bean's Pin Cushion

In the days prior to having my own sewing studio, I used our ten foot dining room table. At the end of a sewing session I either had to put it all away or at least push enough away from one end so we could eat. Fabric was stored in just about every room, every cupboard, trunk, shelf and most of the dining room chairs. I even had 28 large shopping bags full of fabric stored in our downstairs shower. Now, all the fabric is stored on wall to wall shelves that are easily accessible, and that dining room table is now in my sewing room. At the end of the day I can leave everything just where it is so when I start back the next day there is no searching for what I put away. The only problem I seem to have is that my arms are not long enough to reach from the table to the design wall. When I'm trying to pin something up to see how it all goes together, the pins are ALWAYS an extra inch or two away from my reach. I decided to make a pin cushion to hang on my design wall so it would always be handy. While making this quilt for the book I thought perhaps the Auntie Bean's Stalk block would make a charming sunflower pin cushion. I hope you enjoy making this project.

FLOWER: 7"
STEM 19"

Designed and stitched by Lynda Hall

Materials to Gather Together

- 1 fat eighth each of the following colors – red, yellow (middle value to dark), black for the flower and extra pin cushion

- 1 fat quarter total assortment of blacks for the back of the flower and the small black pin cushion

- Cotton stuffing

- 1 fat quarter green for the stem and 2 leaves

- 1 – 12" piece of black 3/16" to 1/4" round cord for hanger

- 1 fat eighth black/red check for two pockets

- Black wool thread

Cutting

Templates on page 70

- Cut 8 black A pieces, 8 yellow A pieces, and 16 red A pieces for the flower base.

- Cut 8 black A pieces for the center pin cushion.

- Cut 2 strips of the green fabric for the stem, 2" x 19" if desired.

- Cut 2 pieces of the red for the pockets, 2" x 10" if desired.

- Leaves for stem – Cut out 4 leaf shapes using the template provided. (Fold green fabric in half, right sides together. Trace around the leaf shape. Cut out the leaf leaving a ¼" seam allowance. The sewing line will be your drawing line.

Assembly

Piece together the Auntie Bean's flower just as you did for the *A Little Porch Time* quilt, except for the corner triangles. Use 8 black triangles, 8 yellow triangles and 16 red triangles to make the large pincushion.

Lay the pieced flower down on some black fabric. Using your ruler and rotary cutter, cut around the block to make the back the same shape. Place right sides together and stitch around the outside edge, making sure you sew it into the octagon shape of the flower. Leave a 1" to 2" opening. Turn right side out and stuff it full. You want this to be firm, but fairly flat. Turn under the raw edge and handstitch it closed.

Piece together a black center for the flower. Cut 8 black A pieces. Sew 4 A pieces together for each half and then sew the halves together.

Lay these pieces down on another piece of black material for the back. Cut around the edges, keeping the octagonal shape. Right sides together, stitch around the edge, leaving at least one inch open for stuffing. Stuff it full; handstitch it closed.

Place this pin cushion in the center of the larger one and handstitch around it. Your flower pin cushion will look dimensional now.

Note: You can stitch on the cord at this point and just hang the flower. However, if you need to have a small ruler and scissors handy, make the stem below with the pockets.

Stem with Pockets

There are times when having a small ruler and/or scissors handy is a plus, so I made the stem with pockets to hold them.

- Cut 2 strips of the green fabric for the stem 2" x 19".
- Cut 2 pieces of the red for the pockets – 2" x 10".
- Cut 2 leaves. (*See note on next page under "Leaves.")

Fold under ¼" at each end of the 10" red/black check piece. Hand-stitch across using a running stitch out of black wool thread. Fold each piece in half lengthwise, with the right sides out and press.

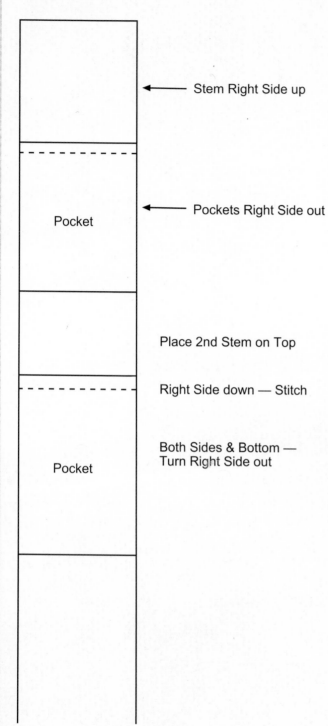

Stem Right Side up

Pocket

Pockets Right Side out

Place 2nd Stem on Top

Right Side down — Stitch

Pocket

Both Sides & Bottom —
Turn Right Side out

Place these pockets (right side out) on top of one green stem, right side up. The top pocket should be 6" down from the top, the second pocket 10" inches down from the top. Place the other stem strip on top, right side facing down, pin all of it in place and stitch down both sides and bottom. Turn right side out and you have a stem with two pockets. Your scissors can go in the top pocket and your 6" ruler can go in the bottom one.

Option: There will be space behind those two pockets and your stem. If you have a long ruler with a hole in one end, you can slip that up behind your pockets and pin it in place. Sometimes we just need a longer ruler and this is a handy place to have one.

Leaves — Make two

*Fold green fabric in half, trace around the leaf shape. Make two of these. Cut out the shape leaving a ¼" seam allowance. Stitch around the shape on the drawing line. Clip several times around the outside edge, being careful not to clip too deep. This will help the edge to lie flat when you turn it right side out. Turn under the raw edge and stitch to the back of your stem where you want them placed. Stitch onto the front as well along the edge of your stem and your leaf to hold the front in place. Attach the stem to the pin cushion.

Hanger

With some black cord, make a loop, stitch it to the flower in the back approximately ½" down from the top. To keep it from flopping forward, also tack each side of the cord closer to the top in the back.

Hang it on your design wall. Everything you need will be at your finger tips.

Enjoy!

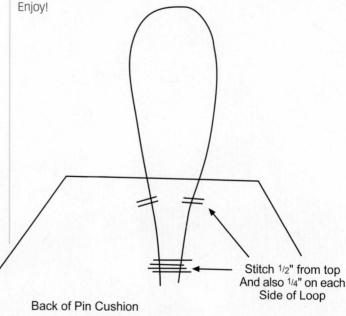

Stitch ¹/₂" from top
And also ¹/₄" on each
Side of Loop

Back of Pin Cushion

Template
S E C T I O N

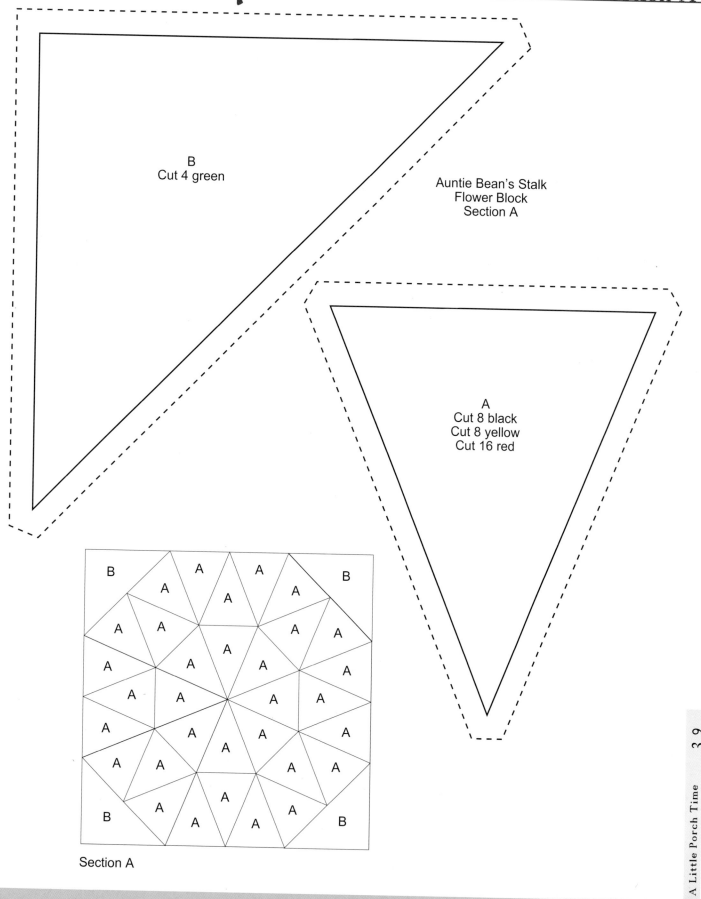

B
Cut 4 green

Auntie Bean's Stalk
Flower Block
Section A

A
Cut 8 black
Cut 8 yellow
Cut 16 red

Section A

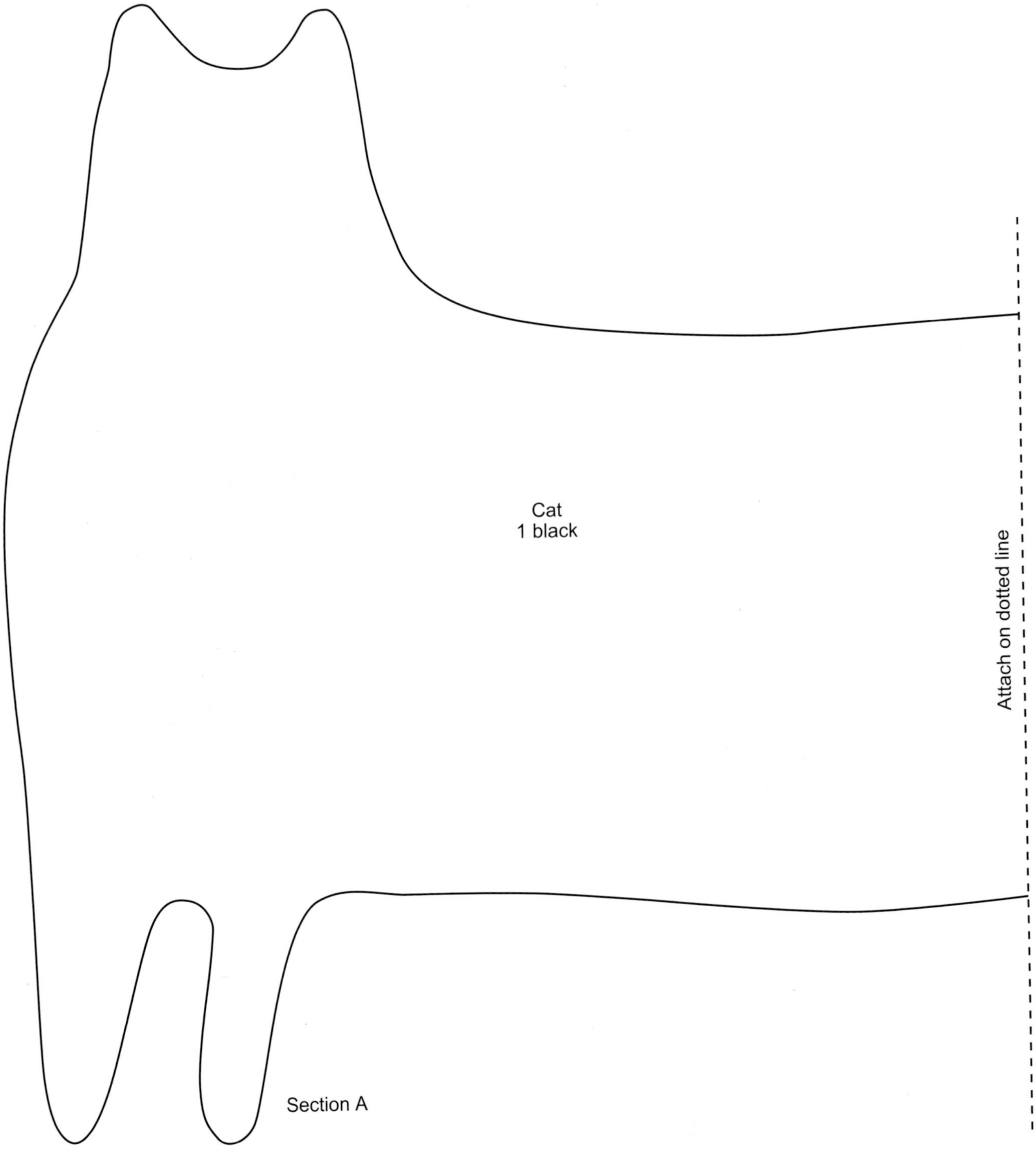

Cat
1 black

Attach on dotted line

Section A

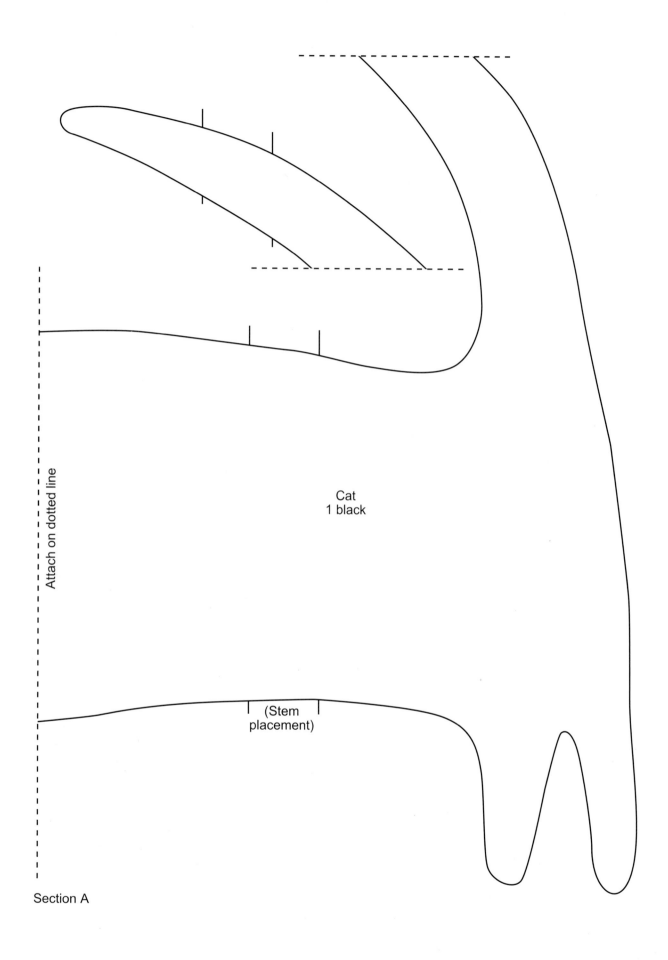

Attach on dotted line

Cat
1 black

(Stem
placement)

Section A

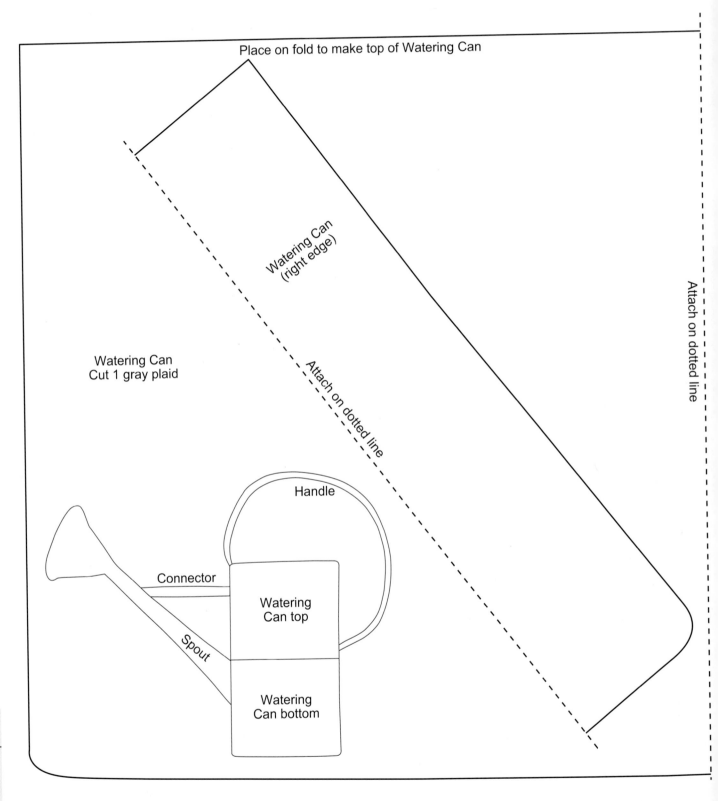

Place on fold to make top of Watering Can

Watering Can
(right edge)

Watering Can
Cut 1 gray plaid

Attach on dotted line

Attach on dotted line

Handle

Connector

Watering
Can top

Spout

Watering
Can bottom

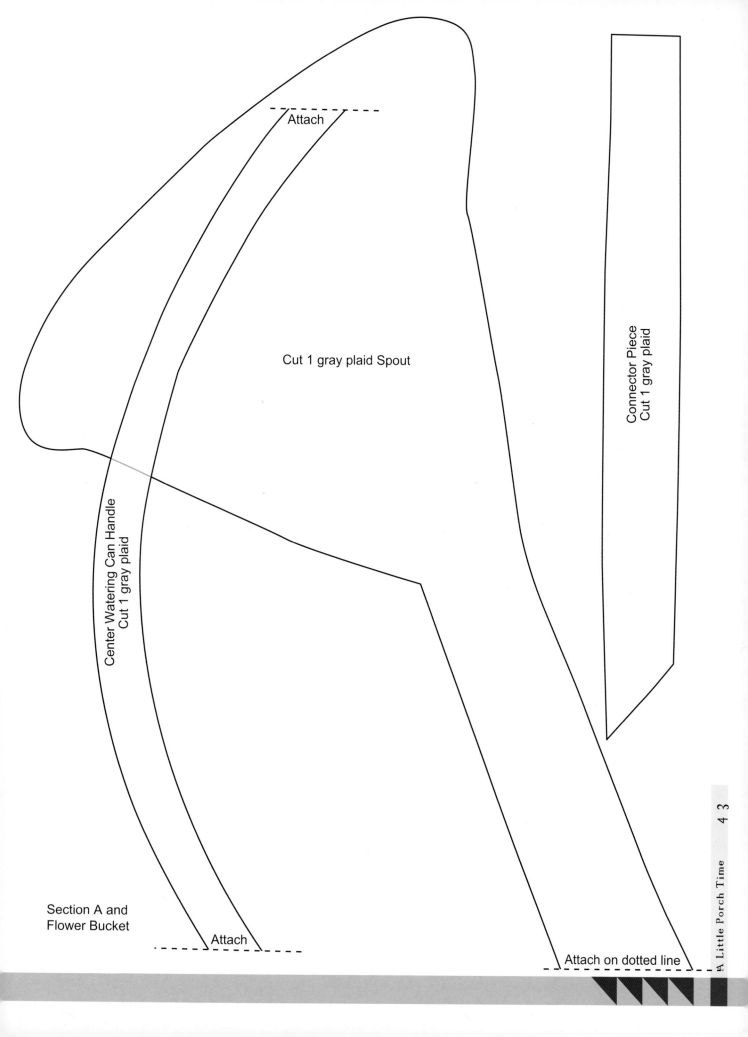

Attach

Cut 1 gray plaid Spout

Connector Piece
Cut 1 gray plaid

Center Watering Can Handle
Cut 1 gray plaid

Section A and
Flower Bucket

Attach

Attach on dotted line

A Little Porch Time and Flower Bucket

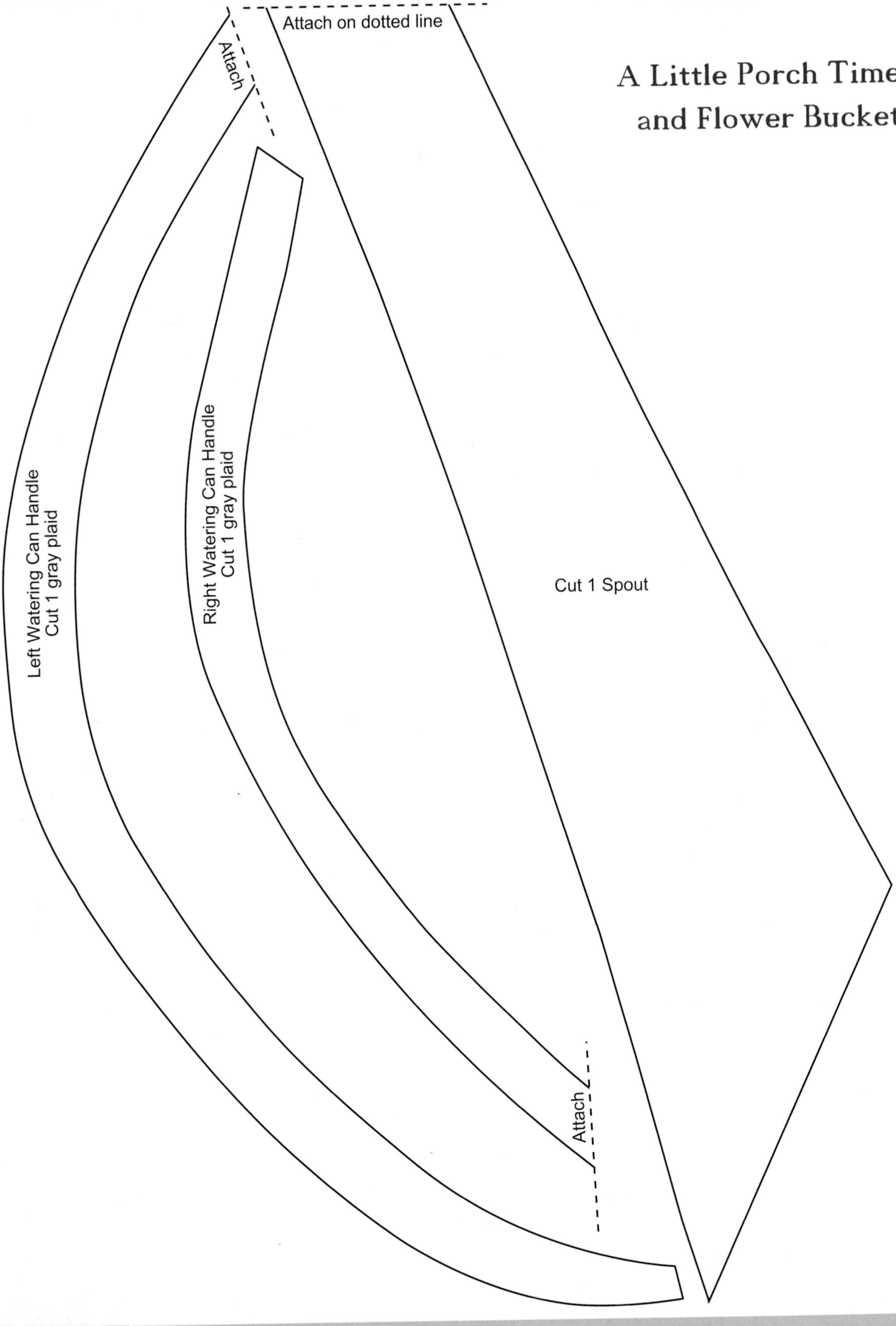
Attach on dotted line
Attach
Left Watering Can Handle
Cut 1 gray plaid
Right Watering Can Handle
Cut 1 gray plaid
Cut 1 Spout
Attach

A Little Porch Time

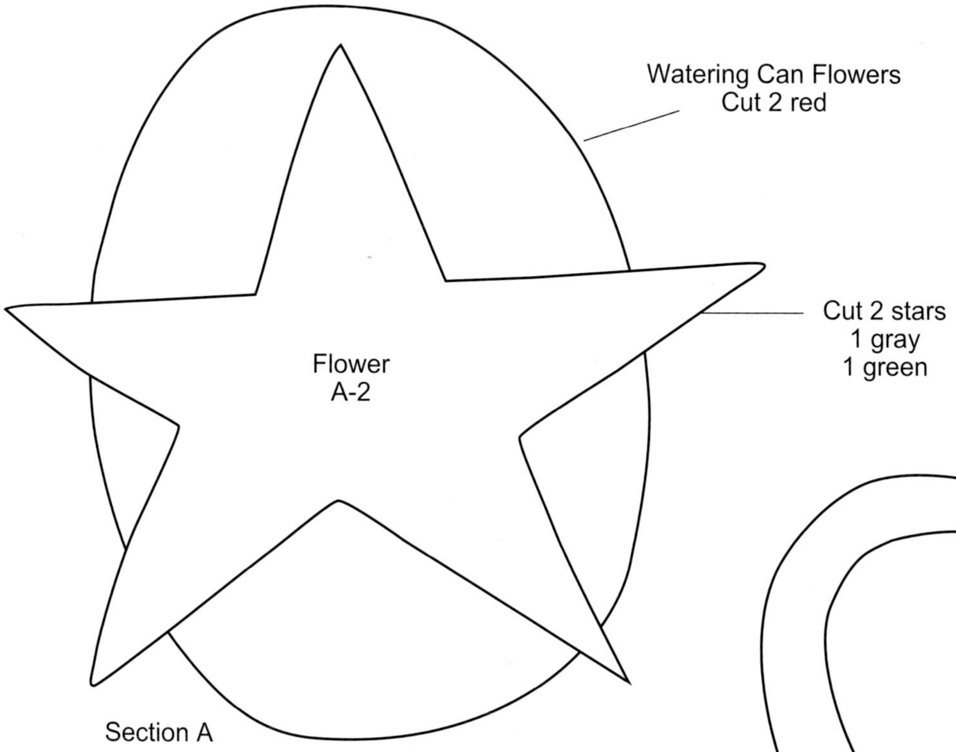
Watering Can Flowers
Cut 2 red
Cut 2 stars
1 gray
1 green
Flower
A-2
Section A

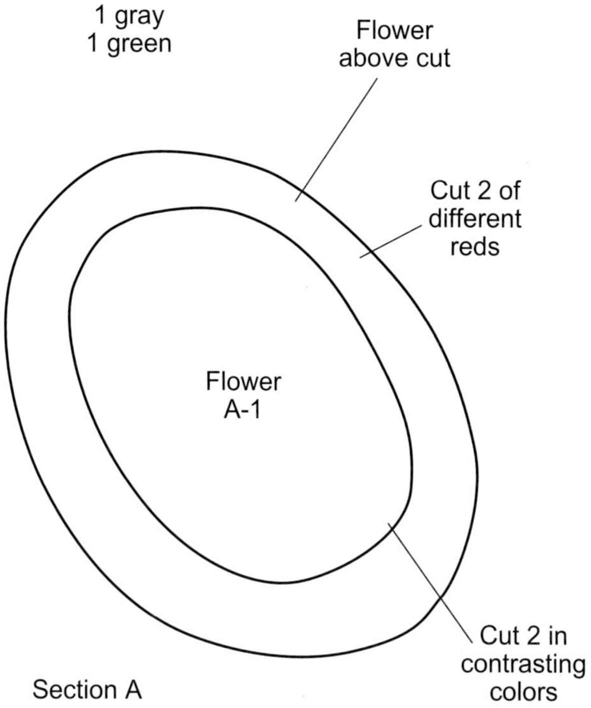
Flower
above cut
Cut 2 of
different
reds
Flower
A-1
Cut 2 in
contrasting
colors
Section A

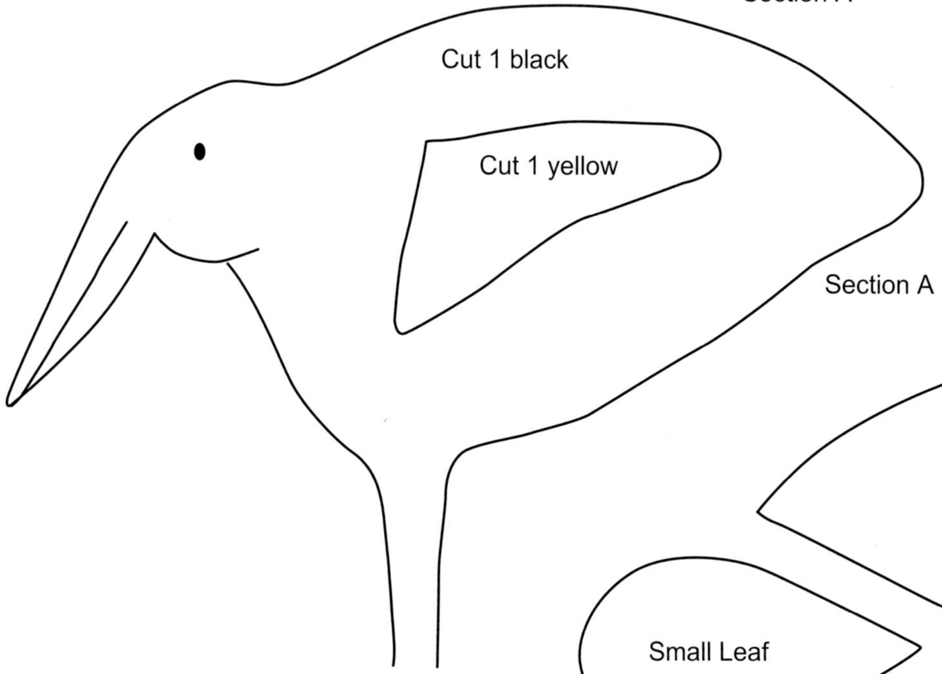
Cut 1 black
Cut 1 yellow
Section A

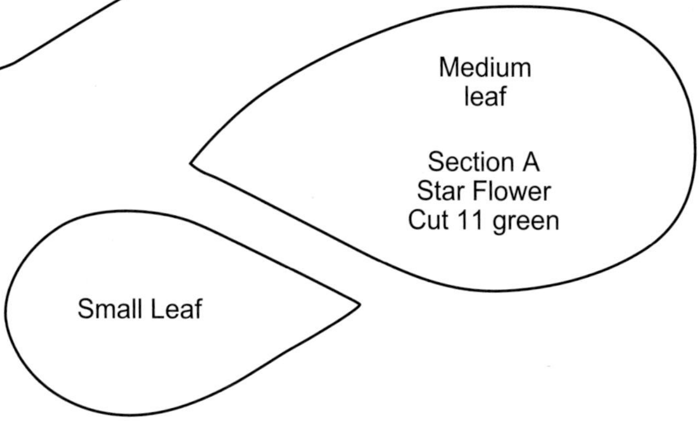
Medium
leaf
Section A
Star Flower
Cut 11 green
Small Leaf

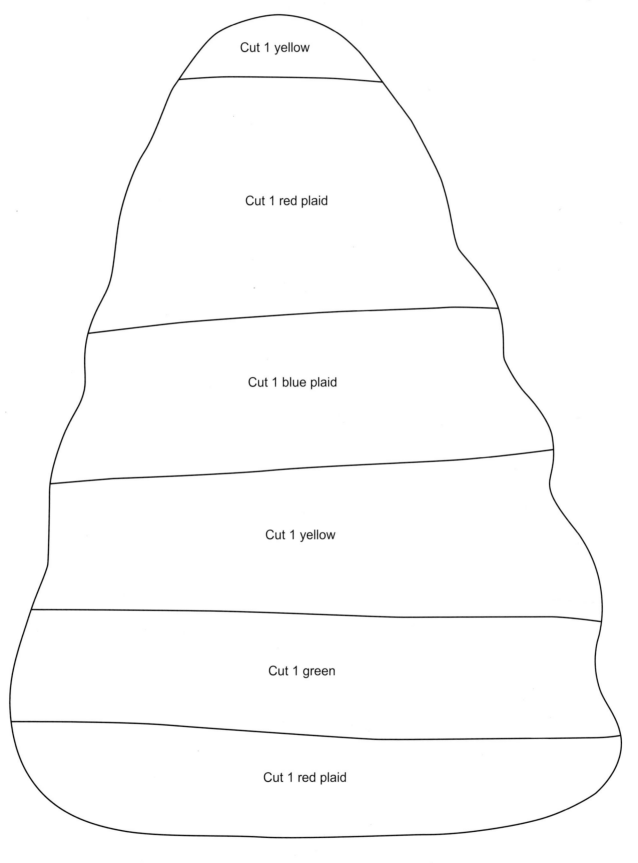

Section B

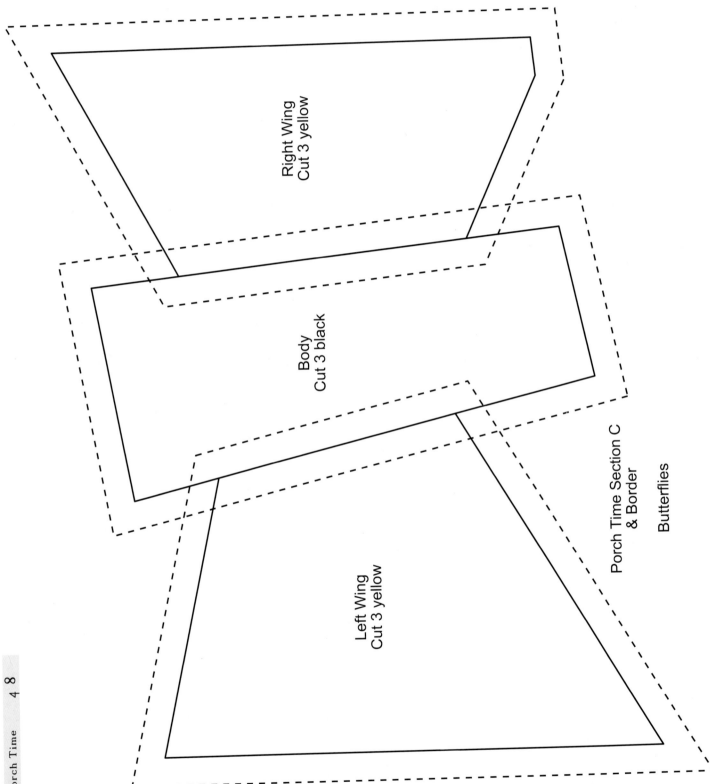

Right Wing
Cut 3 yellow

Body
Cut 3 black

Left Wing
Cut 3 yellow

Porch Time Section C
& Border

Butterflies

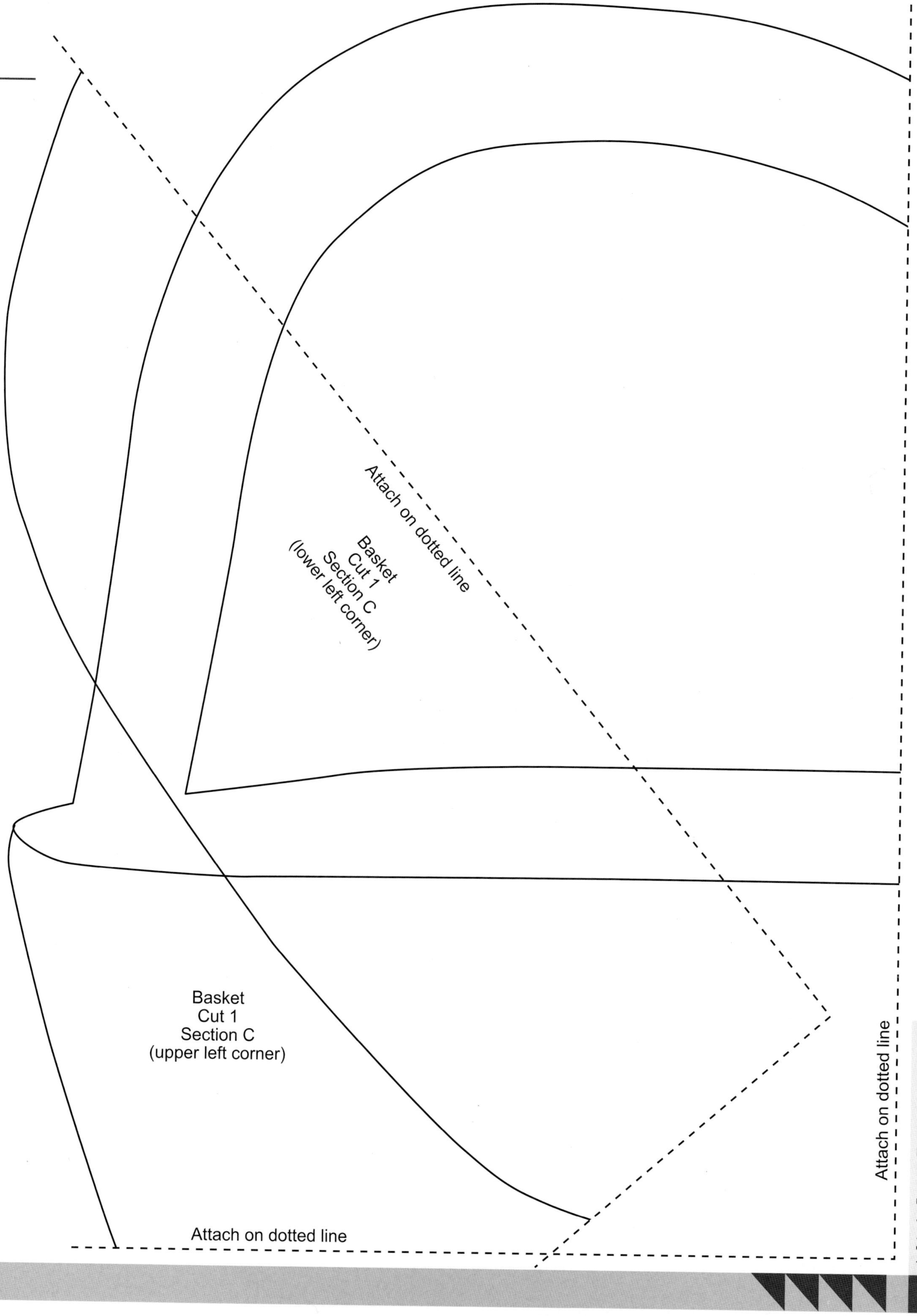

Attach on dotted line

Basket
Cut 1
Section C
(lower left corner)

Basket
Cut 1
Section C
(upper left corner)

Attach on dotted line

Attach on dotted line

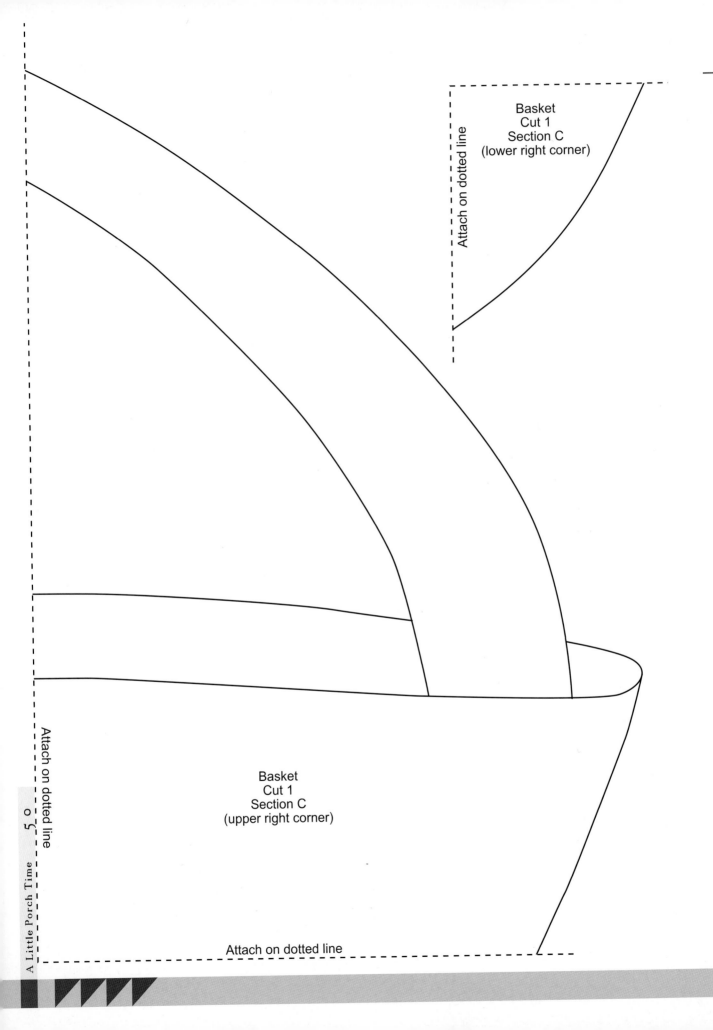

Basket
Cut 1
Section C
(lower right corner)

Attach on dotted line

Basket
Cut 1
Section C
(upper right corner)

Attach on dotted line

Attach on dotted line

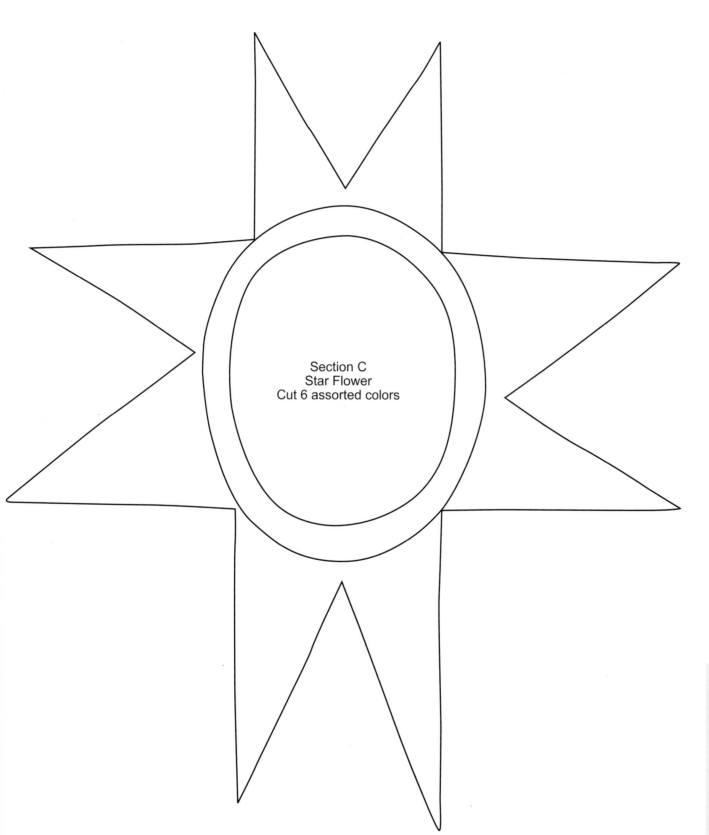

Section C
Star Flower
Cut 6 assorted colors

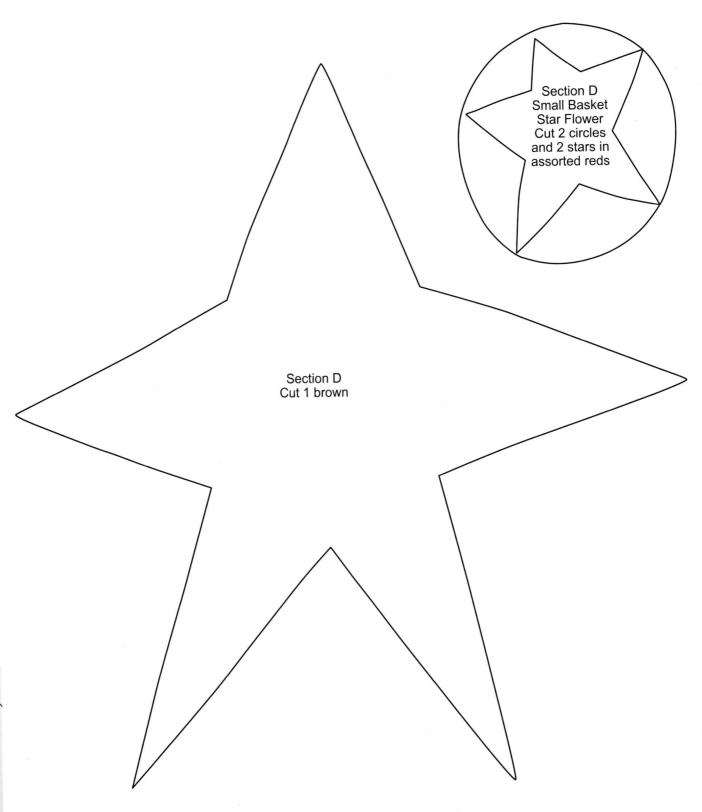

Section D
Small Basket
Star Flower
Cut 2 circles
and 2 stars in
assorted reds

Section D
Cut 1 brown

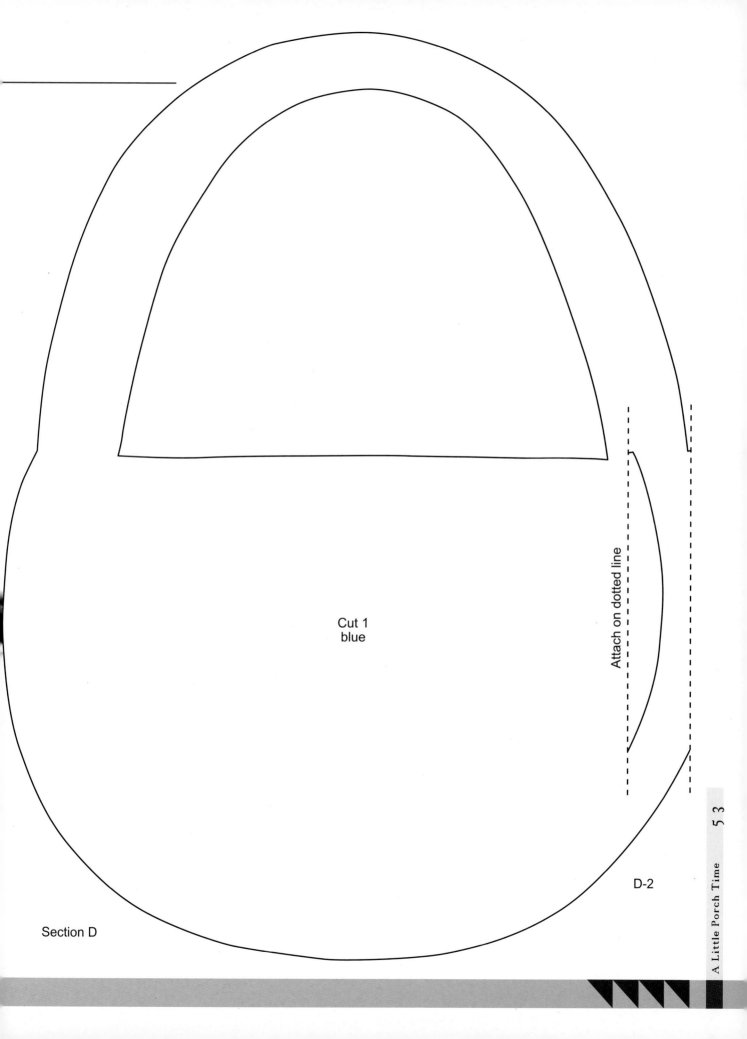

Cut 1
blue

Attach on dotted line

Section D

D-2

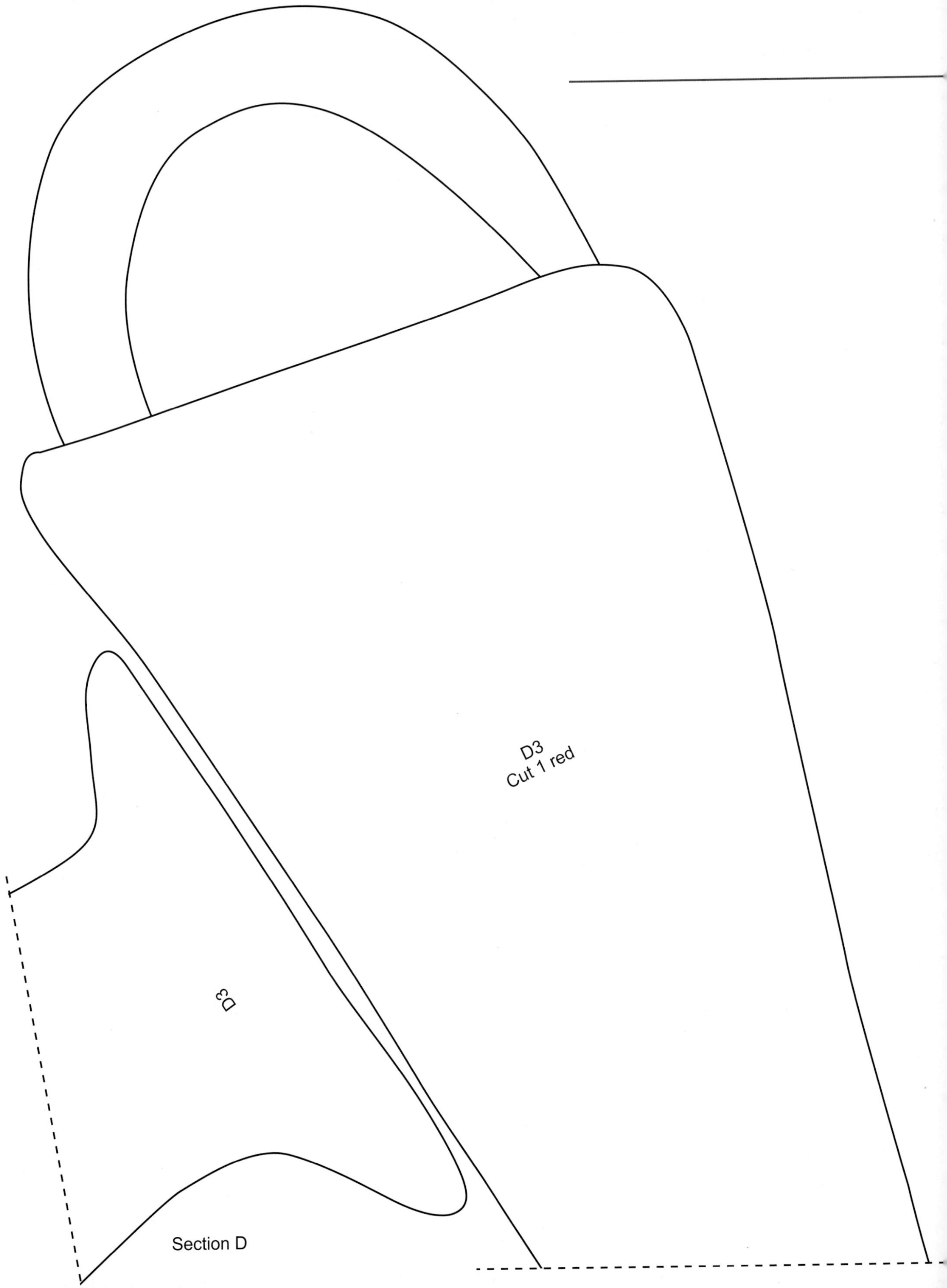

D3
Cut 1 red

D3

Section D

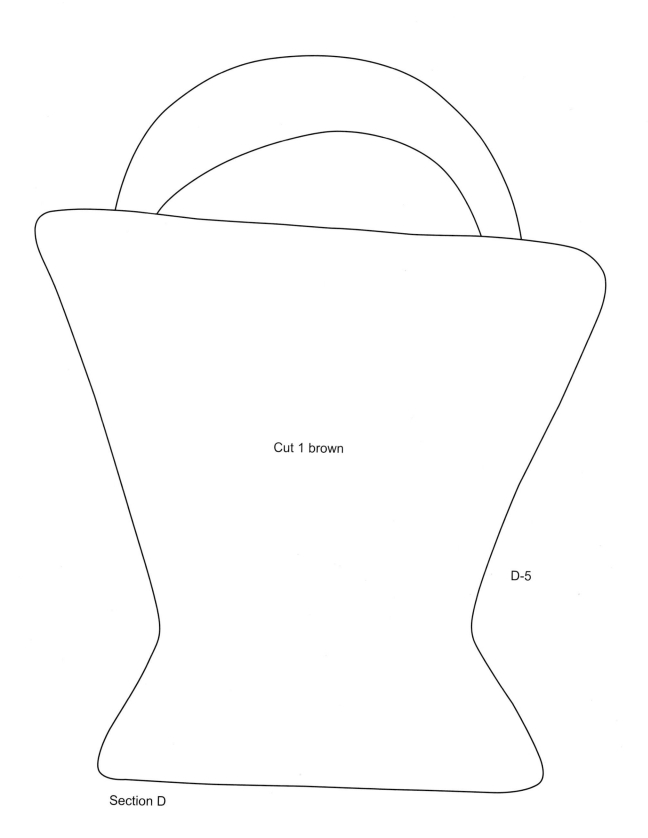

Cut 1 brown

D-5

Section D

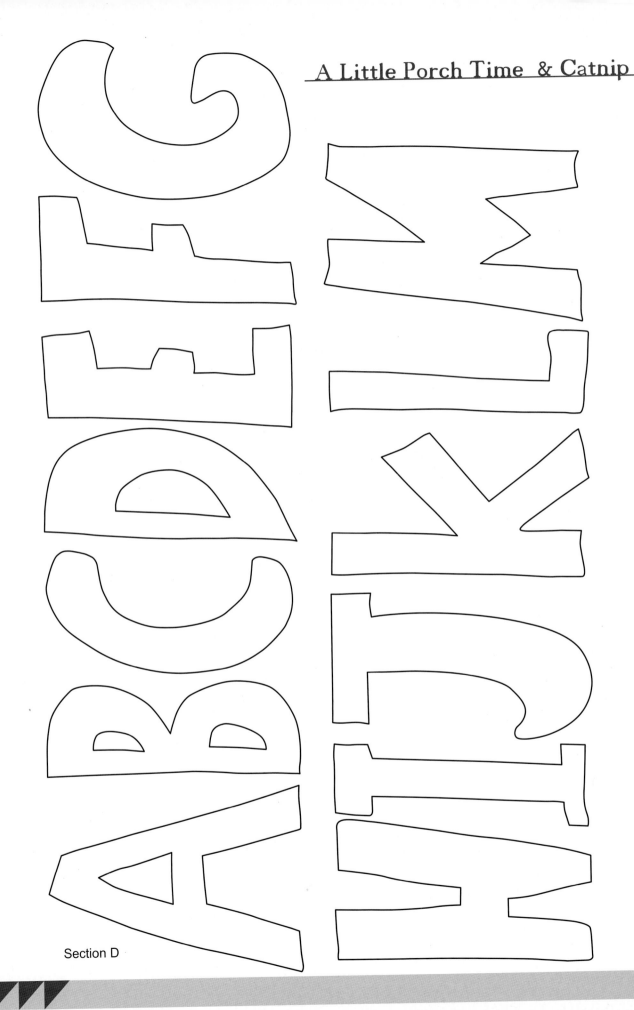

Section D

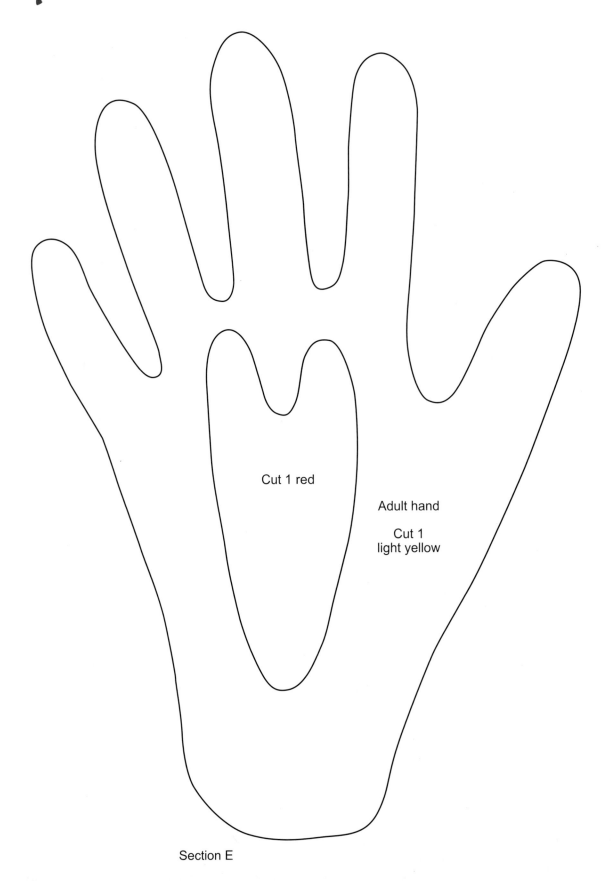

Cut 1 red

Adult hand

Cut 1
light yellow

Section E

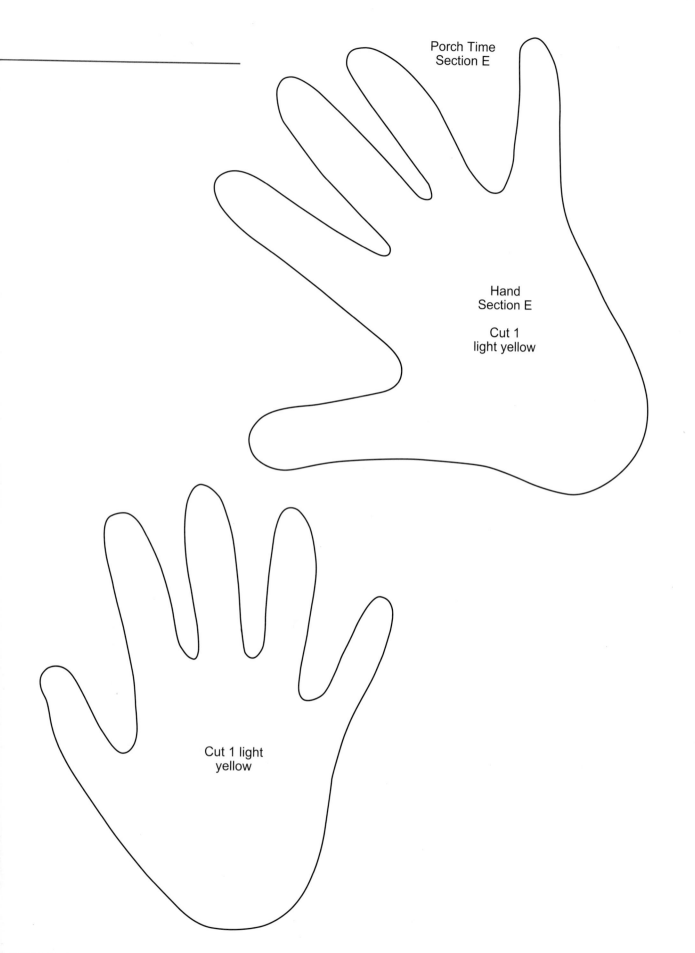

Porch Time
Section E

Hand
Section E

Cut 1
light yellow

Cut 1 light
yellow

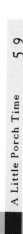

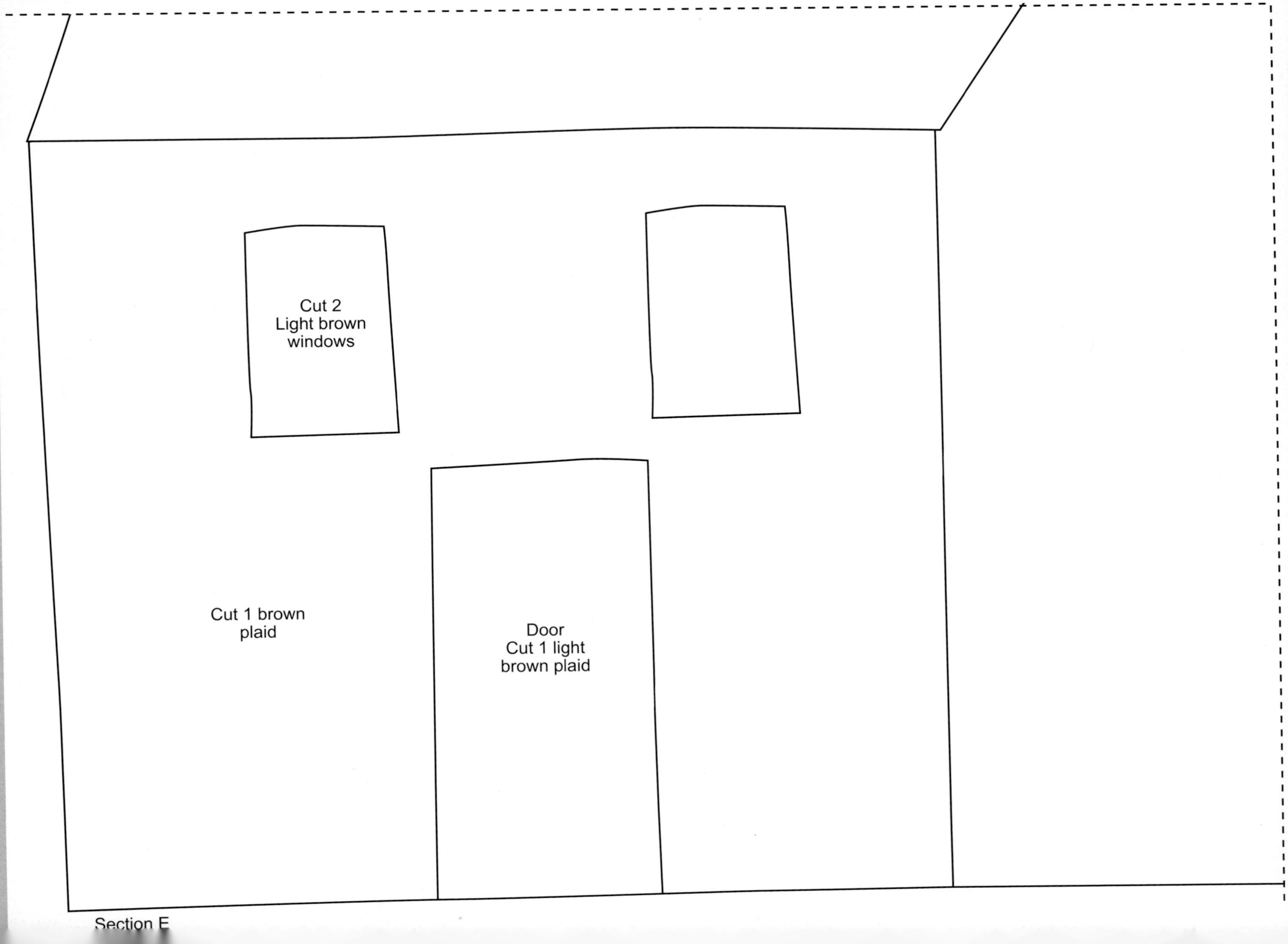

Cut 2
Light brown
windows

Door
Cut 1 light
brown plaid

Cut 1 brown
plaid

Section E

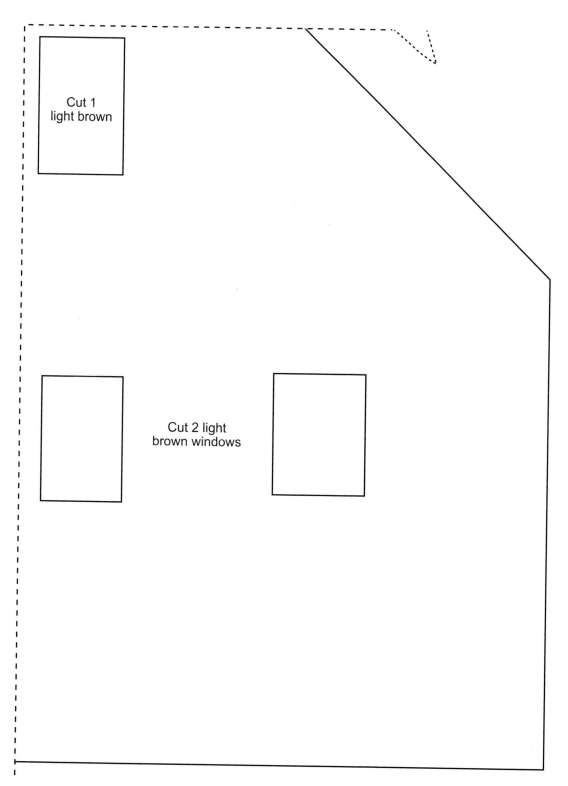

Cut 1
light brown

Cut 2 light
brown windows

Section E

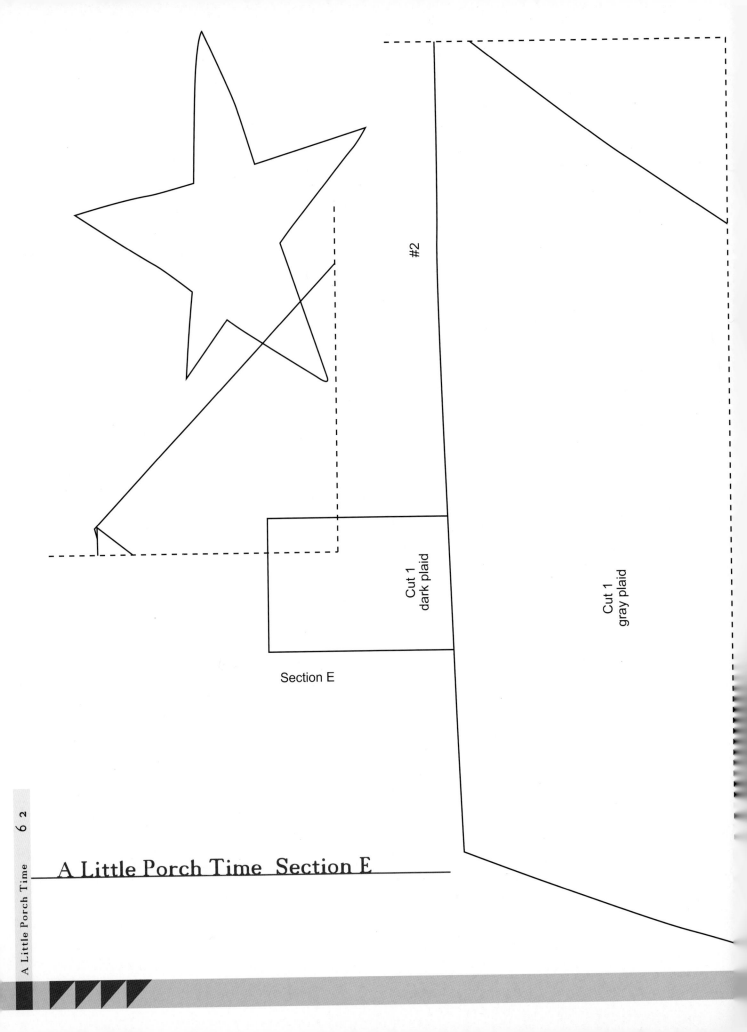

#2

Cut 1
dark plaid

Cut 1
gray plaid

Section E

A Little Porch Time Section E

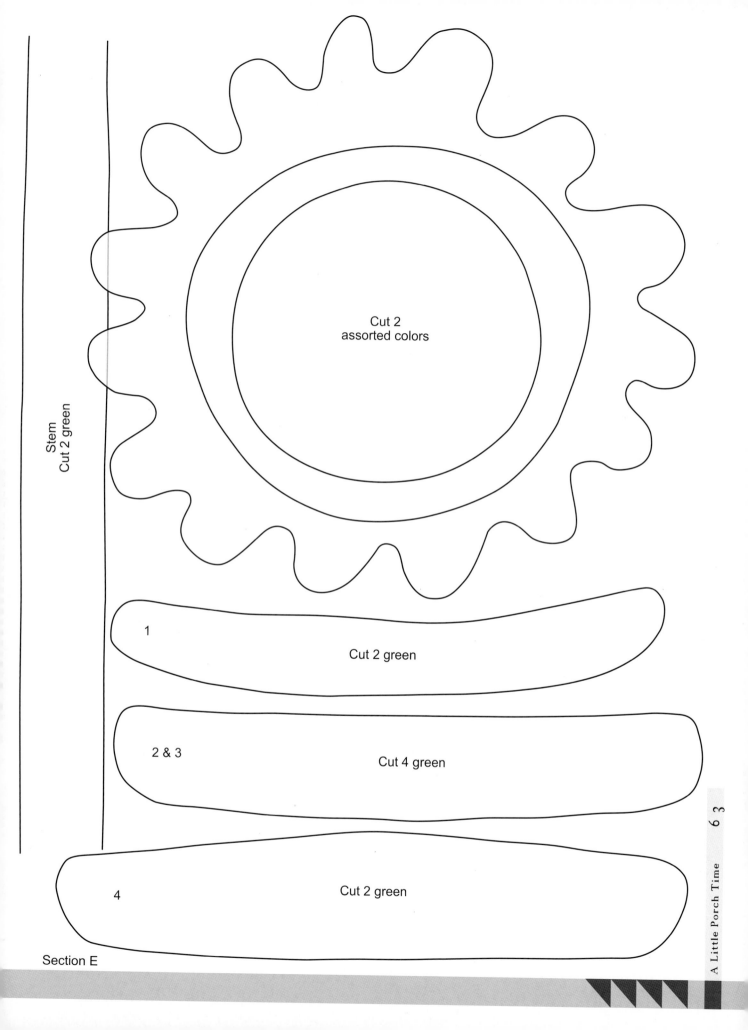

Stem
Cut 2 green

Cut 2
assorted colors

1

Cut 2 green

2 & 3

Cut 4 green

4

Cut 2 green

Section E

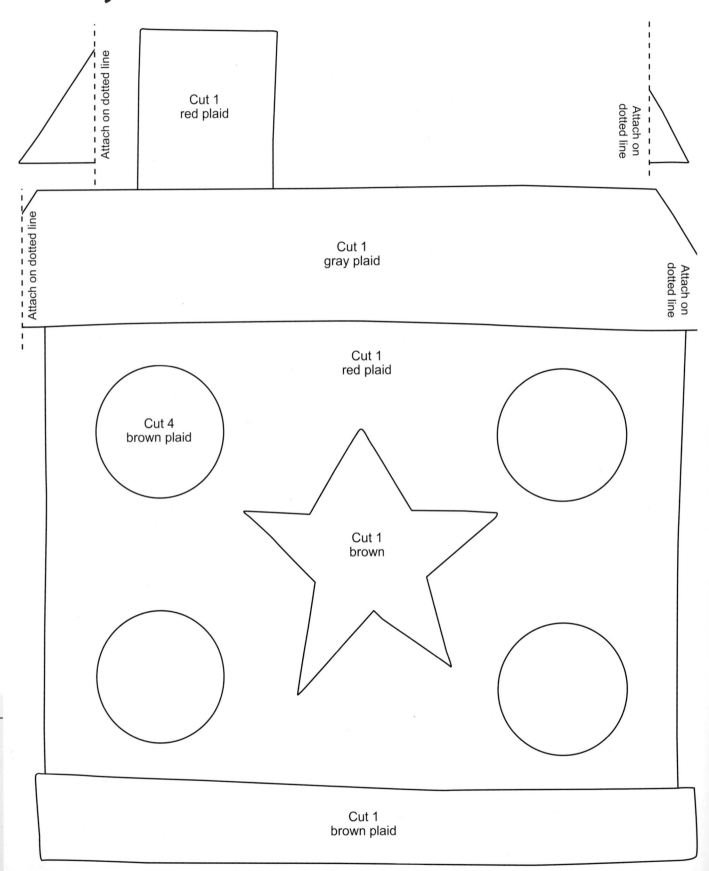

Attach on dotted line

Cut 1
red plaid

Attach on
dotted line

Cut 1
gray plaid

Attach on dotted line

Attach on
dotted line

Cut 1
red plaid

Cut 4
brown plaid

Cut 1
brown

Cut 1
brown plaid

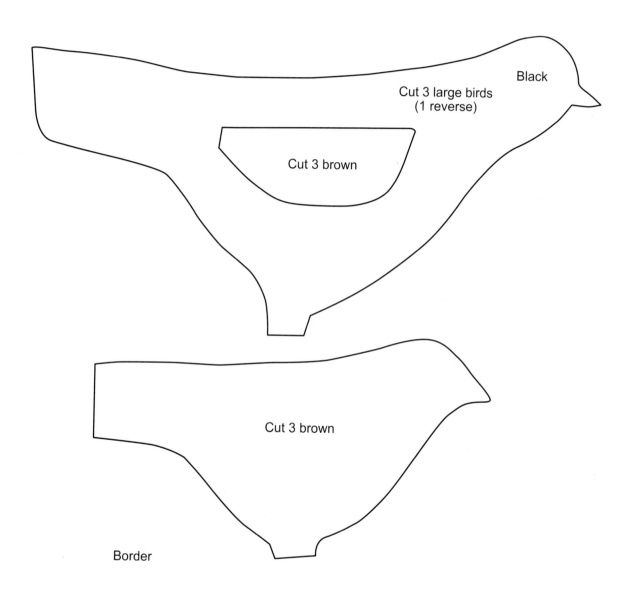

Black

Cut 3 large birds
(1 reverse)

Cut 3 brown

Cut 3 brown

Border

Porch Time Border

Make 3 flowers
of assorted colors

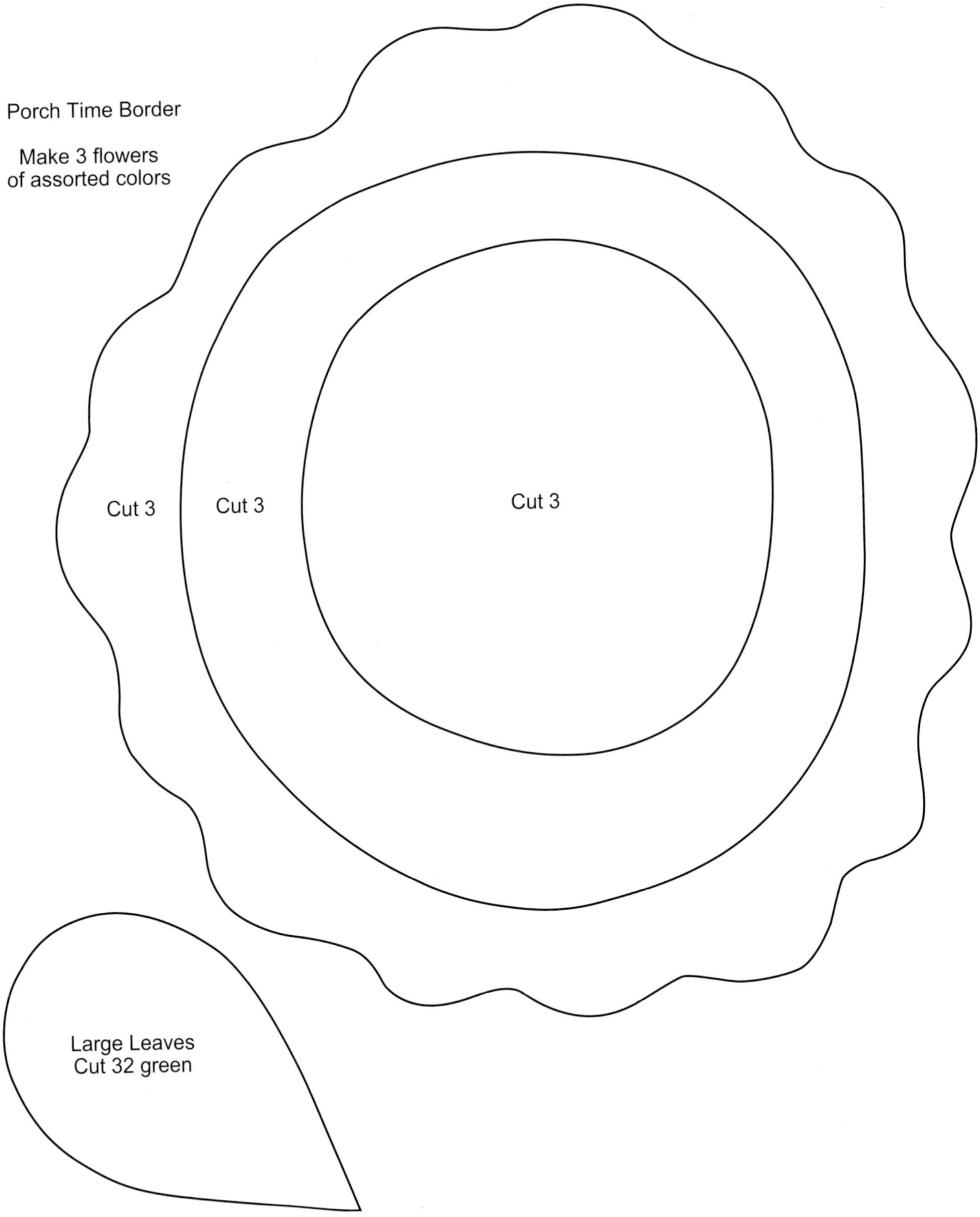

Cut 3   Cut 3   Cut 3

Large Leaves
Cut 32 green

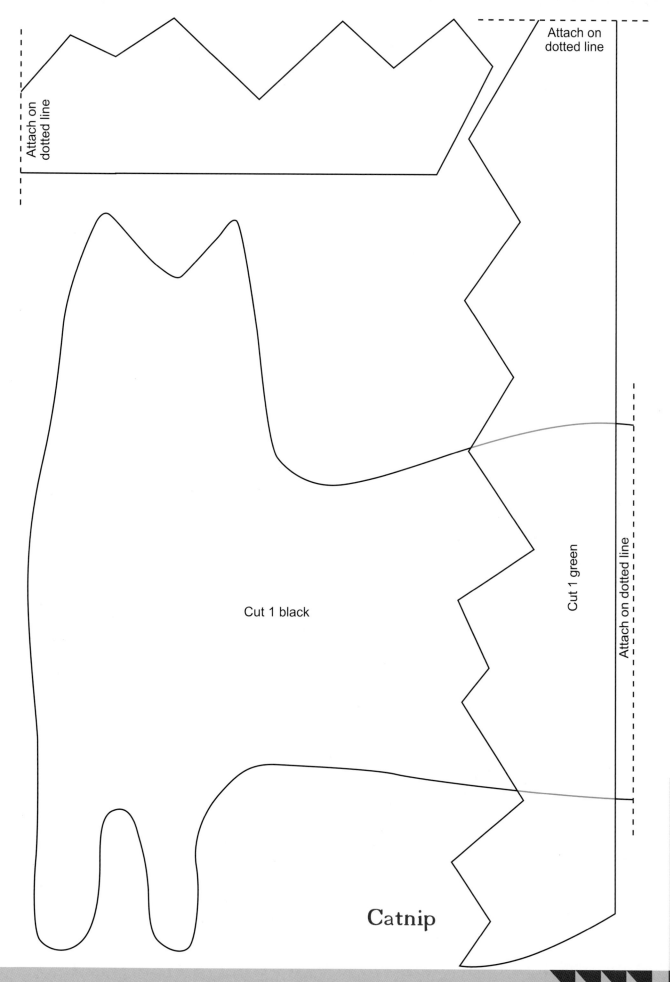

Attach on dotted line

Attach on dotted line

Cut 1 black

Cut 1 green

Attach on dotted line

Catnip

Attach on dotted line

Cut 1
light yellow

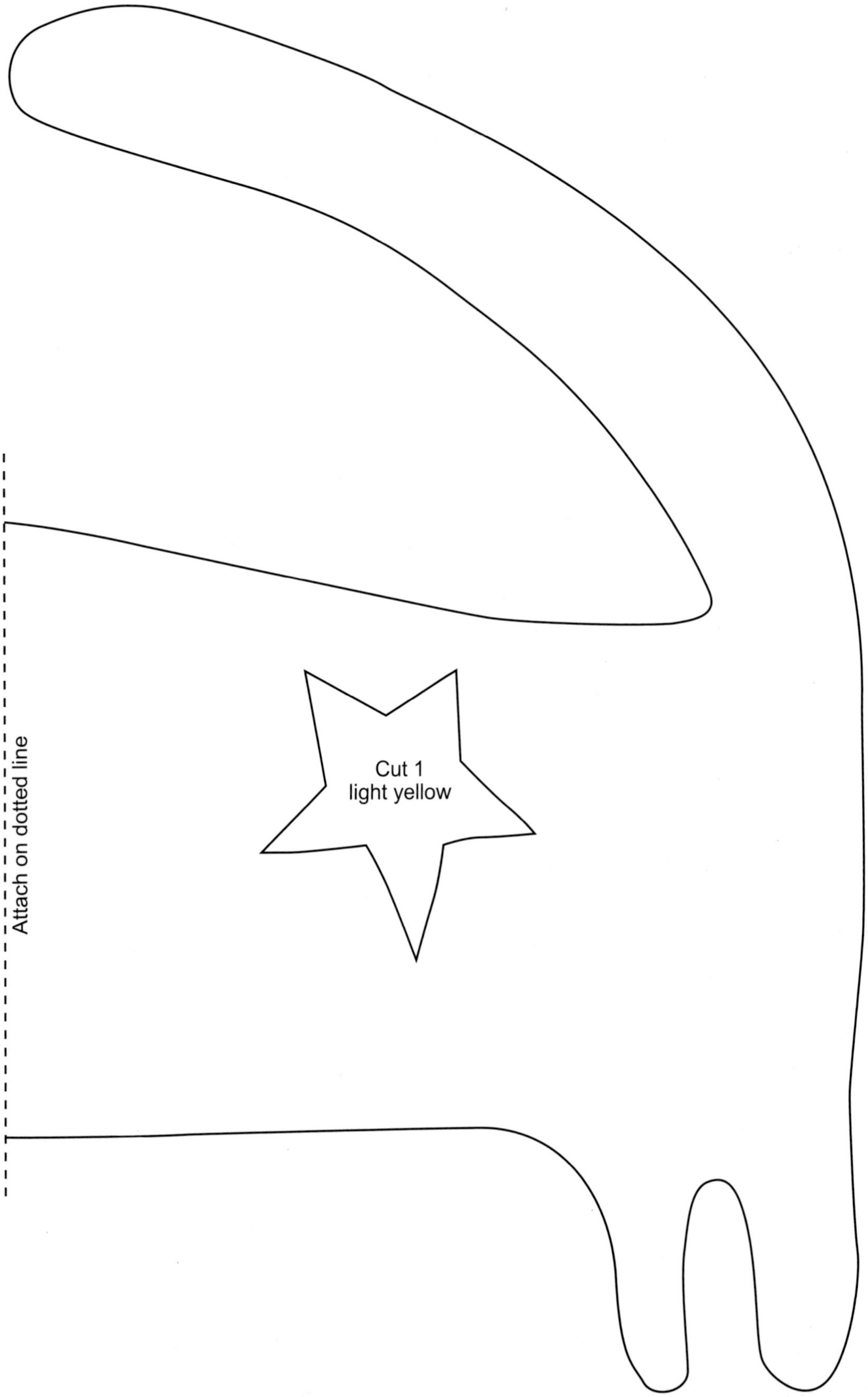

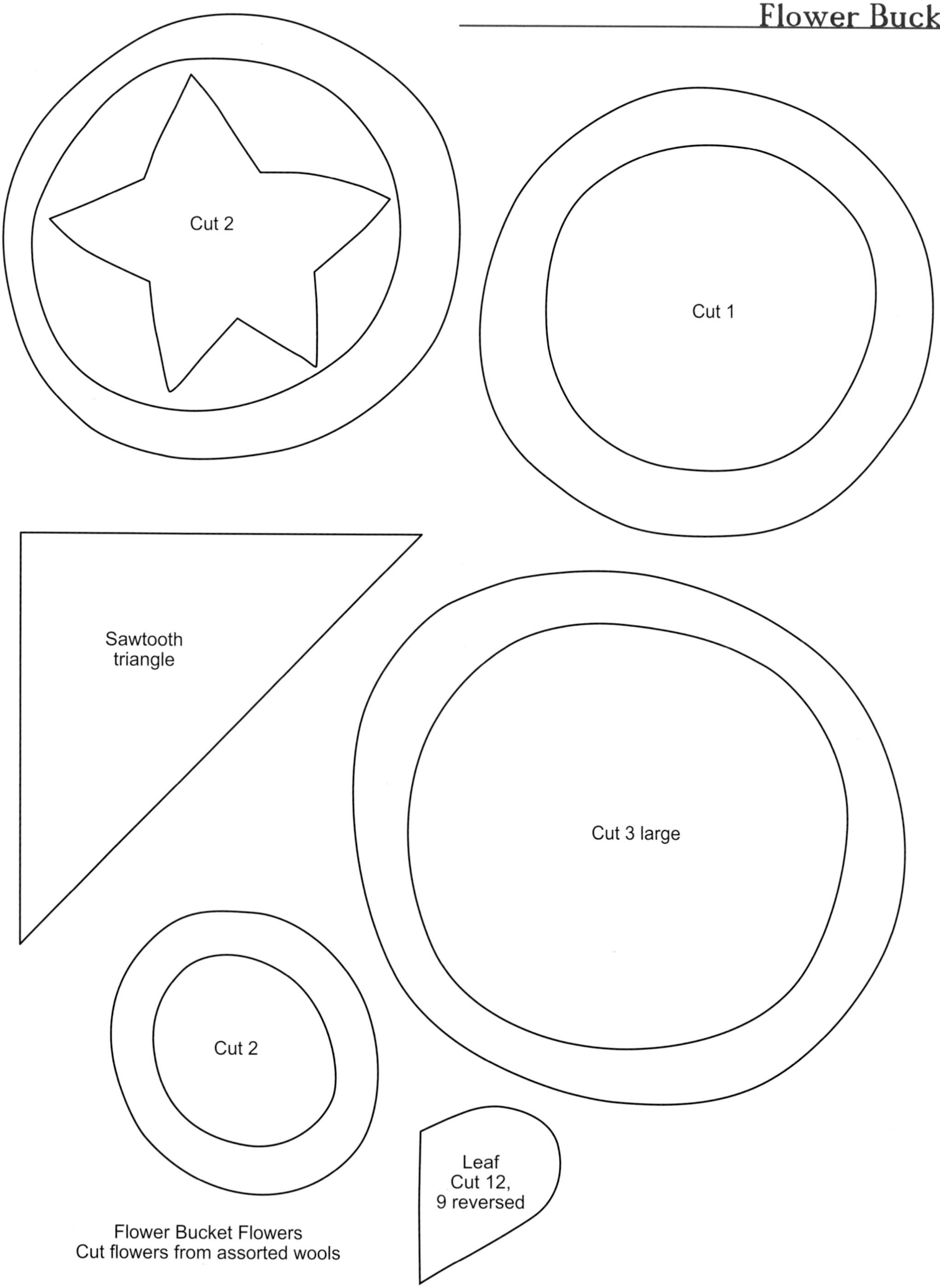

Cut 2

Cut 1

Sawtooth
triangle

Cut 3 large

Cut 2

Leaf
Cut 12,
9 reversed

Flower Bucket Flowers
Cut flowers from assorted wools

Templates Auntie Bean's Pin Cushion

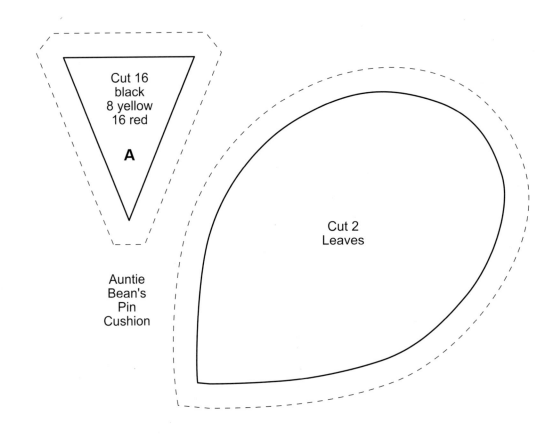

Cut 16
black
8 yellow
16 red

A

Cut 2
Leaves

Auntie
Bean's
Pin
Cushion

Resources

I am asked all the time, "where do you get your fabrics?" or, "what kind of thread do you use?" "I love wool, where do you get yours?" "Tell me more about how you do this", and I get questions regarding color all the time. I encourage everyone to look to their local quilt shops for the fabrics and notions they will need to make the quilts they like – the fabrics, thread, wool and batting used in all the projects in this book can be found locally. If your local shop doesn't carry the items you want; talk with them about ordering for you. I have found that most quilt shops love to accommodate their customers.

I purchase any fabric that makes me happy. I look for colors that are middle value to dark. I like to unroll the bolt about 3 feet, lay it across the shelf in the shop, step back and view it from a distance. I get a better perspective of how it will look doing this. I also look for grayed down fabrics.

Wool sources:

Blackberry Primitives
1944 High Street
Lincoln, NE 68502
www.blackberryprimitives.com

Anita White
12835 Perry
Overland Park, Ks. 66213
913 685-0180
anitahooksrugs@yahoo.com